SpringerBriefs in Law

SpringerBriefs present concise summaries of cutting-edge research and practical applications across a wide spectrum of fields. Featuring compact volumes of 50 to 125 pages, the series covers a range of content from professional to academic. Typical topics might include:

- A timely report of state-of-the art analytical techniques
- A bridge between new research results, as published in journal articles, and a contextual literature review
- A snapshot of a hot or emerging topic
- A presentation of core concepts that students must understand in order to make independent contributions

SpringerBriefs in Law showcase emerging theory, empirical research, and practical application in Law from a global author community. SpringerBriefs are characterized by fast, global electronic dissemination, standard publishing contracts, standardized manuscript preparation and formatting guidelines, and expedited production schedules.

Rhiannon Procktor

The Sexual Offences Act 2003 and Virtual Reality

Applying Criminal Law in the Metaverse

Springer

Rhiannon Procktor
Exeter College
University of Oxford
Oxford, UK

ISSN 2192-855X ISSN 2192-8568 (electronic)
SpringerBriefs in Law
ISBN 978-3-032-10396-3 ISBN 978-3-032-10397-0 (eBook)
https://doi.org/10.1007/978-3-032-10397-0

This Springer imprint is published by the registered company Springer Nature Switzerland AG
The registered company address is: Gewerbestrasse 11, 6330 Cham, Switzerland

Acknowledgements

I am so grateful to have had the support of a great number of people who have made writing this book possible.

Firstly, to Jonathan Herring for sending the email that started it all ("Kind of crazy, but might be worth putting in a book proposal????") and then bearing with me as I continually invaded his emails and office for the following nine months with different ideas and draft chapters. There would be no book without your support, and I feel incredibly grateful to have had you as my tutor for the past four years.

Secondly, to Lauren Fox and Moayed Karar. I could not wish for two better people to have had my back while writing this book. Thank you for challenging me at every opportunity, supporting me, and leaving exceptionally detailed comments on every draft that I threw your way. Here's to a great many more years of sending articles and chapters back and forth and to many more friendly disagreements.

I also owe special thanks to a few individuals who have been incredible over the past few months: in particular, to Isabel Ambrose, Hattie Cooper and Sonya Luchanskaya; and also to Sophie Kitchen, Olivia Clarke, Isaac Dale and Abi Harper for generously giving me your time to listen to presentations and for offering insightful feedback. I also owe a lot to Rachel Taylor and Heloise Robinson at Exeter College for their support and teaching throughout my degree. Equally, to the team at Springer Publishing, particularly my editor Anja Trautmann, who has been amazing throughout.

Finally, and most importantly, to Mum, Merri and Granny. You have all been so supportive of me, not only now but across my entire education, and I could not have done this without you.

September 2025 Rhiannon Procktor
Oxford

Competing Interests The author has no competing interests to declare that are relevant to the content of this manuscript.

Contents

About the Author

Rhiannon Procktor is a graduate of Exeter College, University of Oxford and Université Paris Panthéon Assas. Having had the opportunity to study and live in multiple countries, she enjoys focusing on interactions between technology and law from a comparative perspective. Her work primarily centres on domestic and comparative criminal law, and she is interested in developments in bioethics, neuroscience, artificial intelligence and computer science. rhiannonleprocktor@gmail.com.

Chapter 1
Introduction

On January fifth 2024, the British police force launched the first investigation into the case of a minor allegedly subjected to a "virtual gang rape" whilst wearing a virtual reality (VR) headset.[1] Reactions varied. Comments from a senior police official that "there is an emotional and psychological impact on the victim that is longer term than any physical injuries" were met with a member of the public's scorn-edged scepticism: "Can we focus on real-life crime please?"[2]

There is a small but growing literature addressing the core question presented in cases such as the one described above: are sexual offences perpetrated in virtual and augmented realities "real crimes" deserving of prosecution in the courts of England and Wales?

I ultimately answer this core question in the affirmative.

The law on sexual offences in England and Wales finds statutory footing in the Sexual Offences Act 2003 ('The Act' or the 'SOA 2003'). This statute covers a broad spectrum of crimes, including child rape and other child-related sex offences,[3] abuse of trust cases,[4] trafficking,[5] and many others.[6] The SOA 2003 succeeded the "archaic, incoherent, and discriminatory" 1956 Act of the same name, much of which belonged "to an age before the light bulb or motor car."[7] Change was

[1] Sales (2024).

[2] *Ibid.*

[3] Sexual Offences Act 2003, s.5-s.15A.

[4] *Ibid.* s.16-s.24.

[5] *Ibid.* s57-s.60C.

[6] Including, but not limited to, prostitution and sexual exploitation of family members.

[7] The Sexual Offences Act 1956 had been the foundational document, but provisions were wide-ranging, also found in the Sexual Offences Amendment Act 1976 and the Criminal Justice and Public Order Act 1994. See the comments of the Home Secretary in LGC (2002).

R. Procktor, *The Sexual Offences Act 2003 and Virtual Reality*, SpringerBriefs in Law, https://doi.org/10.1007/978-3-032-10397-0_1

necessary to ensure that the law "[reflected] society's attitudes and [provided] effective protection against today's crimes."[8]

In some ways, the 2003 Act was a step in the right direction: for the first time, the English and Welsh jurisdictions had a general definition of consent, and the Act introduced stronger protections for children. However, the problems it was designed to address persist, and it has not had the intended impact on the number of convictions or de-stigmatisation of sexual offences. Victims of these crimes rarely see justice: of the rapes reported to the police between April 2023 and March 2024, just 2.6% had charges brought by the year's end—let alone a conviction.[9] This statistic is palpably low.[10] Victims are stigmatised and shamed, often leading individuals to feel re-traumatised by the police and justice system.[11] The reluctance to prosecute may be linked to concerns surrounding the protection of the defendant's rights and state interference in private sexual interactions.[12]

The SOA 2003, much like its 1956 predecessor, has found it difficult to move with the times. Technological developments that have transformative effects on social interaction provide an interesting lens through which flaws of the current law can be examined and perhaps amended.

The perception of sexual offences by the public, the legislature, and the judiciary alike is intimately linked to societal norms and marked by changing attitudes steeped in ethical discussion. Sexual relations, like all human interaction, do not occur in some uniform context across the country. They exist, as do we, within the context of our relationships, themselves situated in broader society. This same society has rapidly changed in the 20 years since the Act's inception, partially spurred by an era of profound technological and social evolution. Compared to 20 years ago, there is greater recognition and legal protection of same-sex relationships.[13] For the first time in history, you are just as likely to see a female MP as a male MP walking through the halls of Westminster.[14] The social media platforms that are now pervasive in everyday life were not created until 2006 nor popularised until the late 2000s and early 2010s.[15] In 2004, the same year the SOA came into force, 1.6% of the UK's population owned a smartphone.[16] As of 2025, that number now sits at 95% for all adults aged 16+ in the UK and rises to 98% for UK adults aged 16–24.[17]

---

[8] *Ibid.*

[9] Rape Crisis (2024).

[10] London Victims' Commissioner (2020).

[11] Rape Crisis (2023), see p. 9–13 for an overview.

[12] Olliers Solicitors (2016) and Young (2017).

[13] See, for example, the Gender Recognition Act 2004 and the Marriage (Same Sex Couples) Act 2013.

[14] Cracknell et al. (2024).

[15] For example, Facebook in 2004, Twitter in 2006, Instagram in 2010, Snapchat in 2012 and TikTok in 2016.

[16] Arthur (2014).

[17] Boyle and Barber (2025).

Despite many dystopian challenges, emerging technologies also come with unbridled opportunities. New technology is testing our understanding of nearly every aspect of life, from how we conceive relationships[18] and creativity[19] to property ownership[20] and medical capabilities.[21] This is difficult for the law as it seeks to apply established provisions to novel circumstances. However, it also presents a promising opportunity to radically rethink the law's approach. It is a chance to challenge historically engrained assumptions and ensure that the law is truly adapted and as prepared as possible for the future.

This book is primarily concerned with the English and Welsh jurisdiction. It deals specifically with provisions of the Sexual Offences Act 2003 and relevant domestic case law from this perspective, its influence is most evident in relation to the court's role in statutory interpretation. However, whilst the English and Welsh common law system and its many peculiarities are the primary focus, this analysis may still have some applicability in other jurisdictions.

In terms of technology, I focus on immersive virtual and augmented reality technologies (VR and AR), explored in further detail in Chap. 2. These are represented primarily by the idea of the metaverse. The metaverse has also already been the focus of fierce discussion concerning sexual offences.

After delineating the scope and setting out some key considerations concerning the discussion in Chap. 3, Chap. 4 will turn to the *actus reus* of sexual offences. It will consider issues surrounding the physicality inherent in the 2003 Act; rape, for example, is contingent on 'penetration' as is sexual assault on 'touching'. It is not argued that interactions in the metaverse could be prosecuted as rape under the current statute, but rather that considering developments and user experience of VR, there is a compelling argument to reconsider either the possibility of a legal definition of rape not so exclusively phallocentric, and in any case the assimilation of s.1 and s.2. In addition, it will explore the possibility of new offences to be added to the Act.

Chapter 5 explores the *mens rea* requirement, specifically considering issues relating to how our understanding of reasonable beliefs may differ in virtual environments and some of the challenges relating to mistakes, deception, and gender: issues likely to come to the foreground in an environment where sexual interaction is facilitated through the medium of avatars.

Finally, Chap. 6 briefly considers the wider implications of criminalising sexual offences in virtual reality. Is criminal law the correct venue to deal with these novel situations? How does the analysis presented in this book fit into criminal law more broadly? Equally, are there broader lessons concerning the interaction between law and technology?

---

[18] Gillath et al. (2023).

[19] Zhou and Lee (2024).

[20] See, for example, the recent case of *Thaler* [2023] UKSC 49.

[21] Koujizer et al. (2023).

This book is not intended to set out a comprehensive legal framework that could be put in place tomorrow. Even if I could, the law (unlike various technological developments) is rarely capable of undergoing a rapid 'rewiring' to fix bugs that persist in its foundations. If that were possible, many lawyers and academics would likely be out of a job. This is no such "software update." It is instead intended as a starting point: an overview of the technology as it stands, some ideas for potential reform, and applications of current statute and case law in England and Wales.

References

Arthur C (2014) The death of the featurephone in the UK—and what's next. https://www.theguardian.com/technology/2014/apr/30/featurephone-smartphone-uk-#:~:text=Kantar%20ComTech's%20data%20goes%20back,a%20representative%20panel%20of%20users
Boyle M, Barber S (2025) Mobile Phone and internet usage statistics in the UK. https://www.finder.com/uk/banking/mobile-internet-statistics
Cracknell R et al (2024) General Election 2024 Results. https://commonslibrary.parliament.uk/research-briefings/cbp-10009/
Gillath O et al (2023) How deep is AI'S love? Understanding relational AI. Behavioural and Brain Sciences 46:e33. https://doi.org/10.1017/S0140525X22001704
Koujizer M et al (2023) Implementation of virtual reality in healthcare: a scoping review on the implementation process of virtual reality in various healthcare settings. Implementation Science Communications 4:67. https://doi.org/10.1186/s43058-023-00442-2
LGC (2002) 'Protecting the Public' Strengthening the law on sex offenders and sex offences. https://www.lgcplus.com/archive/protecting-the-public-strengthening-the-law-on-sex-offenders-and-sex-offences-19-11-2002/
London Victims' Commissioner (2020) Rape and the Criminal Justice System: Looking Forward. https://www.london.gov.uk/sites/default/files/2024-03/LVC%20Rape%20Policy%20Paper%202024.pdf
Olliers Solicitors (2016) Defendant Anonymity in Rape Cases: Should the Law Protect the Accused? https://www.olliers.com/news/defendant-anonymity-in-rape-cases-should-the-law-protect-the-accused/
Rape Crisis (2023) Breaking Point: the re-traumatisation of rape and sexual abuse survivors in the Crown Courts backlog. https://synergyessex.org.uk/includes/items/pdf/0750_rcew-breaking-point.pdf
Rape Crisis (2024) Rape and Sexual Assault Statistics. https://rapecrisis.org.uk/get-informed/statistics-sexual-violence/
Sales N (2024) A girl was allegedly raped in the metaverse. Is this the beginning of a dark new future? https://www.theguardian.com/commentisfree/2024/jan/05/metaverse-sexual-assault-vr-game-online-safety-meta
Young G (2017) The Rights of the Victim v the Defendant, Has the Pendulum swung too far? https://www.2harecourt.com/training-knowledge/rights-victim-v-defendant-pendulum-swung-far/#:~:text=While%20those%20who%20practice%20criminal,and%20place%20the%20very%20nature
Zhou E, Lee D (2024) Generative artificial intelligence, human creativity and art. PNAS Nexus 3(3):1–8

Chapter 2
The Metaverse, Virtual Reality and the Law

2.1 Introduction

In October 2021, Mark Zuckerberg, the founder and CEO of Facebook, announced that the company would bring all its apps and technologies together under one brand: Meta.[1]

The focus of this rebranded tech giant?

> To bring the metaverse to life and help people connect, find communities and grow businesses.[2]

Wall Street was not impressed, and Meta has since been "bleeding billions."[3] Reality Labs, Meta's division focusing on metaverse technology, recorded an operating loss of $4.5 billion in the second quarter of 2024[4] and, despite initial enthusiasm, the tech sphere now seems to have refocused on other innovations, such as artificial intelligence.

However, Zuckerberg has not relented. Meta released the Quest 3 on the 10th of October 2023: a VR headset developed for home use.[5] They are not the only ones. On the 5th of June 2023, Tim Cook, CEO of Apple, announced the 2024 release date of the Apple Vision Pro: an augmented reality (AR) headset, supposedly ushering in 'the era of spatial computing' which 'seamlessly blends digital content with the physical world'.[6] Other Silicon Valley companies are also interested in the metaverse's possibilities: Nvidia and Microsoft announced a partnership plan to "bring

[1] Meta (2021).

[2] *Ibid.*

[3] Al-Sibai (2023).

[4] Vanian (2024).

[5] Apple (2023).

[6] *Ibid.*

R. Procktor, *The Sexual Offences Act 2003 and Virtual Reality*, SpringerBriefs in Law, https://doi.org/10.1007/978-3-032-10397-0_2

the industrial metaverse and AI to hundreds of millions of enterprise users"[7]; in 2023, Google's parent company poured 39.5 billion dollars into a private equity firm solely to fund metaverse projects.[8]

Excitement about the metaverse is already evident beyond global tech giants. In 2022, the city of Seoul launched its metaverse. Included in its five-year plan are proposals for virtual libraries, dedicated professional spaces, spaces for youth to access mental health services and even access to the mayor's office, which allows citizens to submit a proposal.[9]

Initial scepticism and perceived commercial failure should not obscure the future of this technology. The reality of the metaverse is far broader, and indeed closer, than we may expect.

The aim of this chapter is twofold. Primarily, it seeks to set out an overview of the technology: what *is* the metaverse? There are three overlapping aspects vital to understanding the implications of these technologies: the structure, the user experience and the enabling technologies. The second aim is to set out a brief history of the interaction between sexual offences and virtual reality. Although we have seen a growth in literature in the private law sphere, particularly concerning data protection and intellectual property rights, accounts of the potential impact on criminal law primarily rely on individuals who have come forward about their experiences.[10]

2.2 Defining the Parameters

The term 'metaverse' originated in the 1992 dystopian novel *Snow Crash*, a combination of the words "meta", the Greek word meaning 'after' or 'beyond', and "universe".[11] With the intention that it will reach one billion people within the next 10 years, spanning across professional, social and academic environments, the metaverse promises a future of limitless opportunity and instantaneous social connection uninhibited by physical borders.[12] On a macro level, it is complementary to development towards Web-3[13] and is "going to have profound generational

[7] NVIDIA (2023).

[8] Bradley (2024).

[9] Ibtekr (2023).

[10] See, for example, Valente (2024) on jurisdiction, and Zhang (2023) for comments on the legality of the metaverse in light of EU law on free movement of goods.

[11] Stephenson (1992).

[12] For the purposes of this article's narrow scope, the entangled web of arguments relating to jurisdiction have not been considered. Further discussion on this point is prevalent in literature relating both to public and private law: Mateu et al. (2023).

[13] Web-3 is a shorthand form meaning the third iteration of the internet. Web-1 represented the origins of the internet, Web-2 was it's capitalization through private companies such as Meta, X and Snapchat, and Web-3 represents a decentralized future of the internet, closely connected with

change".[14] However, as is common with developing technologies, this "natural evolution in connection and the successor to the mobile internet" is yet to be conclusively defined.[15]

Simply put, the metaverse is an immersive digital world where people can connect in a variety of different settings, primarily through the medium of avatars: digital representations of themselves. The experience of each metaverse largely depends on its purpose. Some are social and exist to facilitate human interaction, for example, by playing video games or meeting up with friends for a virtual coffee. Others are more specialist, for example replicating the conditions of the operating theatre and allowing medical students to gain surgical experience.

The metaverse is not a single piece of technology; it is the convergence of several different emerging technologies to enable multisensory interactions with virtual environments, people and digital objects.[16]

This book will adopt an expansive definition of the metaverse:

> a perpetual and persistent multiuser environment merging physical reality with digital virtuality. It is based on the convergence of technologies that enable multisensory interactions with virtual environments, digital objects, and people, such as virtual reality (VR) and augmented reality (AR). Hence, the Metaverse is an interconnected web of social, networked immersive environments in persistent multiuser platforms.[17,18]

The rest of this section will outline the main structural aspects of the metaverse: it is decentralised, interoperable and proprietary.

2.2.1 Decentralised

The umbrella term 'the metaverse' may be misleading. The future is unlikely to consist of a single metaverse owned and operated by one private individual or state actor. For example, a metaverse envisioned by social media giants looks exceptionally different to business-oriented models aimed at digitalising the supply chain.[19] Gamers will expect a different user experience to educators and children. Therefore, the metaverse—or, more accurately, the *metaverses*—are likely to be as diverse as the people and companies whose needs they seek to fulfil. "The metaverse" will

blockchain and other crypto technologies. For a comprehensive understanding see: McKinsey and Company (2023).

[14] Alaghband and Ball (2022).

[15] Meta (n.d.) .

[16] Mystakidis (2022).

[17] Supra (Mystakidis 2022).

[18] Virtual reality (VR) is distinct from augmented reality (AR). AR involves the overlay of digital objects in the non-virtual, whereas VR involves the user entering a fully virtual world. For an overview, see: Johnson (2023)

[19] Supra (NVIDIA 2023).

likely consist of a galaxy of different metaverses, each with "interconnected and interoperable experiences."[20]

Equally, these metaverses will have different guiding rules, such as community guidelines, internal regulation or other user-oriented solutions. Decentraland is one of the largest metaverse platforms and is not organised or run by any one entity. Instead, it is "created and owned by its users" and based on open source code allowing any individual to make improvements or host the platform, meaning that it "can never be shut down."[21] The Decentralised Autonomous Organisation (DAO) is a decision-making tool that allows members to discuss and write proposals to be questioned and voted on by the community. If the votes meet a threshold, then the proposal is subsequently approved and enacted.[22] However, the voting system can present problems, as evidenced in 2021 when a vote to ban the name 'Hitler' in Decentraland failed not due to the proportion of votes received (a majority of those voting were in favour of the ban), but as the number of total votes failed to reach the required threshold to pass.[23]

2.2.2 *Interoperable*

Interoperability has been defined as "the ability to interact, exchange and make use of data and resulting information to enable movement, transactions and participation across systems, platforms, environments and technologies."[24] Interoperable metaverses are desirable as they provide the end-user with a sense of continuity from one space to the next, as well as allow different technologies and platforms to be used to achieve a common goal.

2.2.3 *Proprietary*

Due to this interoperability, there will likely be transferable goods and currencies made possible through blockchain technologies.[25] For example, if Person A buys an item in the non-virtual world, the retailer may also offer a Non-Fungible Token (NFT), which would work in the metaverse.[26] The customer would then be able to

---

[20] Ball (2021).

[21] Decentraland (2024).

[22] *Ibid.*

[23] Choi and Gierhart (2022).

[24] Li et al. (2023), p. 5.

[25] Supra (Ball 2021).

[26] An NFT is a digital asset that can be owned by an individual. For a more detailed explanation, see: Conti and Adams (2024).

use their purchase in the digital world, for example, style their avatar with the t-shirt that they are wearing in the non-virtual. Equally, in Decentraland, users are encouraged to purchase plots of virtual land as NFTs with one company paying a record $2.43 million in 2022.[27]

In short, it will be possible to own goods in the non-virtual world and for these goods to have value in the virtual world and vice-versa.

2.3 Understanding the Experience

There are three overlapping central concepts at the heart of user experience in the metaverse: immersion, presence and embodiment.

2.3.1 Immersion

Immersion primarily refers to the technology's ability to simulate a physical place in a digital environment.[28] As Slater and Wilber argue, immersion relates to the capabilities of the technology; for example, is the visual experience faithful to the physical world, and is there behavioural fidelity between the virtual human's actions, speech and movement to a physical human?[29]

Immersion is scalar rather than absolute: the level of immersion present is dictated and, in some cases, limited by the capabilities of the technology.[30] The greater the fidelity, the greater the sense of immersion.

2.3.2 Presence

Presence distinguishes itself from immersion as it denotes the individual's subjective perception of the virtual environment.[31] Defined as 'the subjective experience of being present in the mediated environment',[32] presence drives the user's perception of a place 'seen' to a place 'visited'.[33]

---

[27] Rosen (2021).

[28] Rzeszewski et al. (2024).

[29] Slater (1999).

[30] Ibid.

[31] Ibid.

[32] Han and Bailenson (2024), p. 3.

[33] Supra (Slater 1999).

The literature has identified multiple types of overlapping presence achieved in VR technologies. It is possible to refer to the spatial presence of an individual: their ability to meaningfully interact with space as if they were there.[34] Equally important is co-presence, which refers to the presence in a virtual environment where individuals are "accessible, available, and subject to" one another.[35] Another form of presence, self-presence, is closely linked to the idea of embodiment discussed below.

Achieving a high sense of presence is commercially beneficial as higher levels have been shown to increase customer satisfaction with the experience of VR[36] and have been shown to play a large role in retaining customers and influencing their perceptions of brands.[37]

2.3.3 Embodiment

Embodiment refers to the individual's feeling of being present in the virtual environment as a body.[38] In VR, this is commonly through the medium of an avatar: an electronic image that represents and may be manipulated by the user.[39] Kilteni, Groten and Slater define embodiment by reference to three subcomponents: the sense of self-location, the sense of agency and the sense of body ownership.[40] In short, avatar embodiment is when an avatar is experienced as the user's biological body.[41]

The importance of this embodiment cannot be understated in the user experience:

> VR is part of a wider context in which our bodies and lives are enmeshed with the digital; the body is critical in all our engagements with the digital as we are embodied agents in the world, and the digital and our embodied activity act as a co-creator of our world (even if that world is virtual).[42]

Through embodiment, the user can meaningfully interact with the world surrounding them and give them a way to enact their agency within the virtual space.

This avatar-user relationship is not unilateral. As highlighted by Yee and Bailenson, the plasticity in the appearance of our online interaction is a fundamental part of any meaningful online identity.[43] Offline, individuals must spend thousands

[34] Supra (Rzeszewski et al. 2024).

[35] Bulu (2012), citing Goffman (1963), p. 22.

[36] *Ibid.*

[37] Cowan et al. (2023).

[38] Dooley (2024), pp. 43–44.

[39] Merriam-Webster (n.d.) 'Avatar'.

[40] Kilteni et al. (2012), pp. 375–377.

[41] Ibid. p. 375.

[42] Evans and Rzeszewski (2020), p. 27.

[43] Yee and Bailenson (2007), p. 272.

in surgery costs, clothing, gym memberships and the like to change the way that we appear. Online, it is as simple as a few quick clicks.

Yee and Bailenson investigated the impact of avatar representations on human interaction through the lens of self-perception and deindividuation theories and discovered a phenomenon they termed 'the Proteus effect'.[44] They argue that in online environments, avatars "are not simply a uniform that is worn, [they are] our entire self-representation", which act as our primary identity cue, subconsciously influencing our behaviour online.[45] As a result, individuals are more likely to conform to the stereotypes of their avatar's appearance:

> Or more precisely, in line with self-perception theory, they conform to the behaviour that they believe others would expect them to have.[46]

Yee and Bailenson's results have been replicated across a range of both physical and 'character' attributes.[47] The Proteus effect has been cited as the reason why users with an athletic avatar reported a lower level of perceived exertion after exercise and were associated with a lower heart rate during exercise than individuals without an athletic avatar[48]; or why there is a link between avatars dressed in Klu Klux Klan uniforms or black cloaks and user aggression.[49]

It is important to note that such embodiment is not automatically achieved using a headset but equally depends on the surrounding virtual environment and senses of presence and immersion.[50]

2.4 Associated Technologies

As alluded to at the beginning of this chapter, the metaverse is not a singular piece of technology. The combined sense of immersion, embodiment and presence is achieved through a variety of technologies, including virtual reality, augmented reality, 5G, artificial intelligence and haptic technologies.[51]

---

[44] Deindividuation is defined as "an experiential state characterized by loss of self-awareness, altered perceptions, and a reduction of inner restraints that results in the performance of unusual and sometimes antisocial behaviour. It can be caused by a number of factors, such as a sense of anonymity or submersion in a group." American Psychological Association (2018).

[45] Supra (Yee and Bailenson 2007), p. 274.

[46] *Ibid.* note, however, that the underlying theoretical basis remains inconclusive in the academic literature, for an overview, *infra* (Coesel et al. 2024).

[47] Coesel et al. (2024).

[48] *Ibid*, p. 3.

[49] Peña et al. (2009).

[50] *Supra* (Coesel et al. 2024), p. 3.

[51] Supra (Ball 2021).

2.4.1 Head Mounted Displays (HMDs)

HMDs are commonly associated with VR due to their increasing presence on the market. Also known as 'VR glasses' or 'virtual reality headsets', HMDs are a variation of a computer monitor which "[attaches] straight to your head and present visuals directly to your eyes…and your peripheral vision as well."[52] They have been used in both commercial contexts, in the case of the Meta Quest and Apple's Oculus, and military contexts, typically in the form of a helmet or goggles.[53]

2.4.2 Haptic Technologies

Haptic technologies are those that stimulate the user's sense of touch. They have notable benefits within a therapeutic context[54] and a commercial context[55] and are often viewed as an integral feature of developing virtual reality technologies.[56]

Their eventual necessity is often explained by reference to their impact on user experience, and their adoption forms an essential part of the distinction between past and future iterations of the internet. As Lanier argues, "'[i]f you can't reach out and touch the virtual world and do something to it, you are a second-class citizen within it … a subordinate ghost that cannot even haunt."[57] It is this ability to interact with the virtual world that plays a role in engaging its users, increasing its commercial viability.

Haptic products are already on the market or in production. Take the Teslasuit.[58] This "full body haptic feedback system" retails for thirteen thousand dollars and uses "electro muscle stimulation (EMS) and transcutaneous electrical nerve stimulation (TENS) to simulate a range of real-life feelings and sensations".[59]

Other products in development range from haptic gloves to headsets equipped with ultrasonic transducers capable of simulating even the delicate sensations of drinking water from a fountain or walking through a spider's web.[60] Japanese company H2L is already revolutionising the gaming market, introducing haptic wearables which "aim to enable humans to share sensations, such as weight and

---

[52] Virtual Reality Society (n.d.) 'Head Mounted Displays (HMDs)'.

[53] DevX (n.d.) 'Head Mounted Display'.

[54] *Ibid.*

[55] West (2024).

[56] Wiederhold (2023).

[57] Lanier (2017), p. 129.

[58] Not associated with Elon Musk.

[59] https://teslasuit.io/products/teslasuit-4/.

[60] Supra (Wiederhold 2023).

resistance, with other people and with robots through patented muscle displacement sensors."[61]

Eager users are already availing themselves of this technology. The company OwO sells a haptic shirt retailing at 150 euros, which promises to help users "live the game" by simulating everything from insect bites to the recoil of a machine gun or a light breeze.[62] Many gamers are interested in trying the technology for themselves, often fascinated by the potential to transform gameplay for the everyday user: "the way your entire playstyle flips and the actual fear of even basic enemies just [because] they can cause you actual pain. I want to try this so f****n bad man."[63]

The adult entertainment industry is another that is exploring the commercial utility of VR technologies. A prominent player in this industry is Forbes' 2019 "Adult VR App of the Year" VIRO Playspace.[64] According to their homepage, they are "the world's first haptic driven social space where touch is encouraged, playfulness is required, and privacy guaranteed."[65] Users can "sync" sex toys at home to the experience provided in the VR space, which ranges from pre-designed and scripted experiences to "Vex Ruby": the world's first "live cam VR girl".[66] VexRuby is a real woman, kitted out head to toe with haptic technology and sex toys that partners can remotely control.

"I'm Alive!" her personality page on the website confirms, 'and real, tracked from head to toe, right down to the fingertips. You can see my actual motions, my real facial expressions, and hear my voice … and all this happens live and in real-time with no pre-recorded movements as we insist on making everything as genuine as possible."[67] In 2022, the same company launched LewdTube LLC: a platform designed 'by performers, for performers' to allow individuals all over the world to create their own 'Vex Ruby' and make money through popular camming websites.[68]

Such platforms are becoming more accessible through the greater accessibility of teledildonics, an advanced type of sex toy.[69] At the less advanced end of the spectrum, it is possible to connect a vibrator to a mobile app, allowing another user to control it from anywhere in the world. On the more advanced end, it is possible to buy a "Twerking Butt" to be used in conjunction with VR pornography, featuring "multiple twerking patterns, customisable rhythms, massage speeds, and a realistic simulated body heat of 98.6°F".[70]

---

61 WIPO (n.d.).

62 OWO (n.d.).

63 @MegamanStarforce2010 https://www.youtube.com/watch?v=lHc-oQrkEH4.

64 Formerly 'Virtual Romance Club/ViRo Club'.

65 https://viro.club/overview.

66 https://viro.club/vexruby/#personality.

67 https://viro.club/vexruby/#personality.

68 https://store.steampowered.com/app/2247990/ViRo_Live_Studio__Adult_Streamer_Tools/.

69 Knowles (2017); Cam Soda is another platform which allows users to connect with performers through teledildonic toys.

70 *Ibid.*

Aylo, the Canadian-owned company responsible for the likes of Pornhub, Brazzers and several other brands, is the leading manufacturer and distributor of adult entertainment in the world.[71] In the space of 2 months in 2016, the launch of Pornhub's VR portal went from 30 videos to over 2600 and gained more than 500,000 views.[72] Currently, it does not offer the option to interact with other users, although, given the development of technology and other sites such as LewdTube, this is a likely possibility in the future.

Overall, a wide variety of industries and companies are starting to turn to the metaverse to improve user experience through this greater sense of immersion, often facilitated using haptic technology. Leading players in the adult entertainment industry are already driving innovation at the genesis of metaverse technology.

The metaverse as it currently operates is often distinguishable from the non-virtual world. However, we ought to be careful not to dismiss claims on this basis alone. There need not be a full assimilation of the non-virtual and the metaverse to manifest a realistic sense of presence, immersion and embodiment. Events online do not have to be entirely indistinguishable from their offline counterparts to have physical repercussions.[73]

2.5 The Non-autonomy of the Virtual

There is often a distinction drawn between the 'virtual' and the 'non-virtual'. However, this is a false dichotomy which is "fundamentally misleading, if not mistaken."[74] Malpas argues that this distinction fails to recognise the 'non-autonomy' of virtual worlds. Materially, he argues, they are dependent on infrastructure existing in the everyday and not in the virtual: Meta's Horizon Worlds are not powered by virtual servers using virtual energy, they are reliant on global data centres. Equally, our interactions are played out in the "real world" in real-time, whether that is through the click of a mouse or the physical enactment of these movements whilst wearing a VR headset. The individuals acting in this virtual world are individuals whose agency is exercised from the offline world, and our attachment to these virtual personas is often rooted in the way that the virtual interacts with an individual's everyday lives, be that for recreational purposes, creative purposes, financial gain or social connection.[75] The interdependence of the virtual and the everyday is equally recognisable in the understandings and significance attributed to events and images:

---

[71] Morris (2023).

[72] Garnham (2017), p. 9.

[73] Further discussion of these physical repercussions, particularly as they relate to sexual interaction, will be explored further in later chapters.

[74] Malpas (2008), p. 1.

[75] Ibid, p. 3.

> The content that is embodied in the virtual—the narratives it presents, the significance of the individual events and elements that occur within it, and the meanings that can be attached to the images and texts that it generates—is always dependent on the everyday world in which the virtual is embedded.[76]

However, such a dependence between the virtual and the everyday does not automatically entail that the virtual is a replica of the everyday. Avatars with tails, fire-breathing powers and the ability to fly are not off-limits in the metaverse. This ability to be creative and have new experiences is one of the greatest advantages of virtual reality, especially as it relates to education and creativity.[77] It is a mistake, however, to assume that this is a satisfactory reason for rejecting the view that the virtual is a separate entity from the everyday. Instead, the virtual does not represent a divergence from the physical constraints of the everyday but a divergence from the experiential constraints of everyday life as imposed by the laws of science.[78]

Summing up his argument, Malpas reiterates:

> "…the non-autonomy of the virtual means that the virtual is causally and contentually interconnected with the everyday. This not only means that virtual domains such as Second Life are causally and contentually dependent on the everyday, but that they are also causally and contentually effective on the everyday—that they have real, everyday consequences. In this way, recognising the non-autonomy of the virtual also enables recognition of the reality of the virtual—a reality evident within the everyday.[79]

It may then seem counter-intuitive that this book will continue to use the labels 'virtual' and 'non-virtual' to distinguish actions in virtual reality and those not. This is primarily for pragmatic reasons. The first is that virtual/non-virtual is the most intuitive way to communicate this difference. The second is that alternatives, such as physical/non-physical and meta/non-meta, are either equally misleading or too narrow. As much of this book will argue, there are "physical" aspects to interactions in VR, therefore, to term it 'non-physical' is misleading. Equally, although the metaverse will be frequently used as a case study and is the most obvious place in which criminal conduct may occur, it is not necessarily the only one: there may be other forms of virtual and augmented reality that will fall into this category, especially as technology is in a constant state of development. There may, however, be some offences which merit the prefix "meta" in their current forms, as they are only currently possible in the metaverse.[80] However, these relate to specific offences and not the distinction as a whole. What this book instead advocates for is a nuanced understanding of 'virtual' in the context of emerging technologies. It is not a synonym for imaginary, delusional or "not real" but descriptive of a state of affairs in a specific context.[81]

---

[76] *Ibid.*

[77] See, for example, Capatina et al. (2024).

[78] Supra (Malpas 2008), p. 3

[79] Supra (Malpas 2008), p. 9.

[80] See, for example, McGlynn and Rigotti (2024).

[81] Indeed, there are some communities for whom the virtual is the everyday and becomes the primacy world of interaction, see for example, Boellstorff (2020).

2.6 The Metaverse and the Law

2.6.1 Origins

In 1993, Julian Dibbell detailed his experience of 'A Rape in Cyberspace' after witnessing the "cyberrape" of a woman in the online community of LambdaMOO.[82] This community, allowing interaction between user-programmable avatars, terrorised by one 'Mr Bungle' which described graphically non-consensual acts to be performed on other avatars described by one victim as capable of causing "post-traumatic stress" and dividing the community on how to approach the situation.[83] He was eventually "toaded"—removed from the game—but returned with a new skin and a new name not too long after, continuing with similar harassing tactics.

This was followed in 2006, with the first investigation by a police force into rape on the platform Second Life, again sparking debate about the existence of cyberrape.[84] Cybersex and harassment are rife in the online community.[85] Popular children's game Roblox has come under increased scrutiny in recent years, especially for reports of "gang-rapes" of avatars operated by children as young as seven[86] and "Nazi sex parties" occurring within the game.[87] In 2020, Roblox estimated that two-thirds of children aged between 9 and 12 in the US use the game.[88]

2.6.2 Current Issues

The debate was once again renewed at the beginning of 2024 when the British police launched the first investigation into a rape reportedly occurring on Meta's VR platform.[89] The alleged offence occurred whilst the victim, a girl under the age of 16, was surrounded and assaulted by several male adult avatars in the virtual world.[90] This follows reports published by international security and policing agencies into the potential criminal applications of the metaverse, including the potential for sexual offences and harassment and reports from individuals of their adverse experiences.[91] However, the efficacy of measures such as Meta's safety bubble has been

---

[82] LambdaMOO is a text-based role-playing world.

[83] Dibbell (1993).

[84] Duranske (2007).

[85] Schott (2017).

[86] BBC (2018).

[87] Knowles (2022).

[88] Clayton and Dyer (2022).

[89] Sales (2024).

[90] *Ibid.*

[91] Europol (2022) and Interpol (2024)

complicity in the growth of online crime.[23] Furthermore, the inquest into the death of British fourteen-year-old Molly Russell found that material viewed on social media was likely to have "affected her mental health in a negative way and contributed to her death in a more than minimal way."[24] There are calls for increasing regulation from many spheres, including bills such as the Online Safety Act 2023 and the Stop Addictive Feeds Exploitation (SAFE) for Kids Act 2024, signed into law by Governor Gournades in New York earlier this year.[25]

Similar to the non-virtual, interactions in the metaverse are often dictated by the purpose of the virtual environment. For example, the social norms and expectations present in a child's game or educational experience are going to differ greatly from a metaverse that VexRuby or similar VR cam-girls operate in.[26] The types of expected and tolerated behaviour and interaction will be entirely different. As a result, users in the metaverse exist within different 'digital cultures' depending on the world they choose to enter: the 'netiquette' changes from metaverse A to metaverse B.

The emergence of new "digital social norms" in the current iterations of the internet results from the dynamism and influence of environmental and external factors, including offline culture, on human interaction online.[27] For example, the type of language and expression used on LinkedIn is vastly different to that used on Instagram. One review found that "netiquette is situative, influenced by contextual factors such as the platform, power imbalances and social relationships."[28]

As a result, communication of consent and consent itself may not be identical to the way that the courts are used to identifying it. We ought to be open to a flexible approach, taking into account the range of human expression and social norms present in the virtual world.

5.3.2 General Challenges

The fact that each metaverse has its own community guidelines and social norms, written or monitored not by the state but by private profit-driven companies, is cause for concern.

There is potential to argue that, as metaverses will not usually only be accessible in one jurisdiction, it may be worthwhile having a baseline definition of consent to clearly delineate what constitutes consent and what does not. However, difficulties arise if we allow the companies to delineate the boundaries of consent themselves.

[23] McQue (2024).

[24] North London Coroner's Service (2022), para 4.

[25] New York State Senate (2023).

[26] See discussion on Vex Ruby in Ch. 1.

[27] Heitmayer (2023).

[28] *Ibid*, p. 15.

questioned, and they will be challenged with increasing frequency, given the growth in interest and accessibility of VR.[92]

There is a clear distinction between the text-based platforms in operation when conversations around cyberrape and sexual harassment began 20–30 years ago and the types of technology available now. Being targeted in a virtual world where the user is immersed, present and embodied opens the door to a different type of wrong, distinct from text-based communication offences.

2.6.3 *Hacking Concerns*

Some academics have already started to consider the unique challenges presented by sexual interaction in the metaverse. There are growing questions over the existence and operation of 'dark verses': virtual worlds operated by private actors without limitations or guidelines in a similar way to today's dark web.[93] Equally, concerns about the potential of hacking abound; the example given earlier of a seven-year-old's experience of gang-rape in Roblox was facilitated by a 'rape script': a piece of code injected by hackers into Roblox servers allowing them to override the game's safety features.[94]

Hacking also allows for different forms of attacks to be perpetrated. For example, overlay attacks are described as when "the attacker takes complete control over the user's virtual environment and provides their own overlay – the input which defines what users see and perceive in a virtual environment."[95] A victim could also be subjected to a 'Human Joystick Attack', where they can be moved to another location or tricked into hitting objects and walls.[96] Such attacks highlight the unique concerns in the context of the metaverse and interaction online more generally.

2.7 The Reality of Sexual Offences in VR

Sexual violence, in all its forms, can cause significant psychological harm in respect of the victim. Some recognition of this fact is found in recent responses to claims for civil damages for psychiatric injury caused by past sexual violence.[97]

Reports of experiences of sexual violence in virtual reality mirror non-virtual responses, as evidenced by Patel's account:

---

[92] Pierce (2022).

[93] Dwivedi et al. (2023).

[94] Tsukayama (2018)

[95] Europol (2022), p. 22.

[96] *Ibid*, at p. 21. For the original paper, see Casey et al. (2021).

[97] See recently, *IMX v L* [2024] EWHC 2183 (KB) and *CAX v PQR* [2023] EWHC 3198 (KB).

> I recently shared my experience of sexual harassment in Facebook/Meta's Venues. Within 60 seconds of joining — I was verbally and sexually harassed — 3–4 male avatars, with male voices, essentially, but virtually gang raped my avatar and took photos — as I tried to get away they yelled — "don't pretend you didn't love it" and "go rub yourself off to the photo".
>
> A horrible experience that happened so fast and before I could even think about putting the safety barrier in place. I froze.
>
> It was surreal. It was a nightmare.[98]

Tonic immobility, or 'freezing' in place, occurs as a result of responsive hormonal changes, primarily in terms of inhibition and release of cortisol, adrenaline and opioid analgesia, resulting in parts of the body that are unnecessary for immediate survival to 'shut down'.[99] The finding by one study that 70% of rape victims in Sweden had experienced this type of reaction was part of what prompted the Swedish reform of sexual offences law, part of a wider drive to encourage victims to come forward and combat the stigma surrounding sexual offences.[100]

As a result, Meta introduced a 'safety barrier' which can be triggered by the user and prevents other users from interacting directly with their avatar.[101] This is to be recognised as progress to the extent that it provides a method to prevent the interaction within a defined space. However, if such a feature puts the user into a "SafeZone", the necessary and rather interesting implication is that the rest of the virtual world that exists is not a "safe zone". Considering that much of the draw of the metaverse is the ability to participate whilst immersed, present and embodied, it would suggest that individuals belonging to groups more susceptible to harassment in the non-virtual will have to avail themselves of the feature. In short, protecting the vulnerable whilst failing to address the problem does not seem an efficient, or indeed "safe", way to go about it.

There is little research available currently on the precise psychological and physiological impacts of sexual offences in virtual reality.[102] Concerning VR's impact on sexual experience and activity, the embodied nature of the metaverse is a key factor in distinguishing its use from 2D erotic material, such as pornographic videos. Multiple studies have found that both physiological and subjective sexual arousal and presence increase using first-person VR with erotic stimuli.[103] If human interaction and experience in virtual reality are intended to mimic "real world" interaction, it is not so absurd to suggest that so too will sexual experiences.

The technology industry cannot at once purport to mimic senses and experiences for profit and, at the same time, deny the adverse experiences as taking things too far. The same unique selling point of the technology should not be used as a reason for disbelief or disregard of survivor's experiences.

---

[98] Patel (2021).

[99] De Heer and Jones (2024).

[100] Batha (2020).

[101] Tabahriti (2022).

[102] This is unsurprising given the emerging nature of the technology. However, the accounts of the victims are exceptionally important under these circumstances and should be accorded great weight.

[103] Milani et al. (2022).

2.8 Ending on a Positive Note

Much of this book focuses on the misuse of VR technology. Like virtually all technology, it presents a great danger if used by bad actors or left without effective regulation. However, it also presents great promise. From new opportunities in the educational landscape to making healthcare more accessible, the metaverse could overwhelmingly reshape human connection and learning for the better. Such positive developments ought to be emphasised at the outset. This is not a book advocating for the criminalisation of the metaverse in general; it is a book about the law on sexual offences as it applies in virtual reality. It encourages embracing the promise of new and emerging technologies whilst keeping a keen eye on potential misuses and the need for an effective and enforceable regulatory framework.

References

@MegamanStarforce2010, Gingas VR (2024) 'YOU can FEEL PAIN in SKYRIM VR—Episode 3'. [Video] https://www.youtube.com/watch?v=lHc-oQrkEH4

Alaghband M, Ball M (2022) At the Edge: the promise and peril of the metaverse. Transcript available here: https://www.mckinsey.com/capabilities/mckinsey-digital/our-insights/the-promise-and-peril-of-the-metaverse

Al-Sibai N (2023) Zuckerberg's Metaverse is Bleeding Billions of Dollars, Documents Reveal. https://futurism.com/the-byte/zuckerberg-metaverse-billions-losses

American Psychological Association (2018) 'Deindividuation', https://dictionary.apa.org/deindividuation

Apple (2023) Introducing Apple Vision Pro: Apple's First Spatial Computer. https://www.apple.com/uk/newsroom/2023/06/introducing-apple-vision-pro/

Ball M (2021) The Metaverse Primer. Accessible at: https://www.matthewball.vc/the-metaverse-primer

Batha E (2020) Rape conviction rise 75% in Sweden after change in the law. https://www.reuters.com/article/world/rape-conviction-rates-rise-75-in-sweden-after-change-in-the-law-idUSKBN23T2R2/

BBC (2018) Roblox blames 'gang rape' on hacker adding code to game. https://www.bbc.co.uk/news/technology-44875920

Boellstorff T (2020) The ability of place. Curr Anthropol 61:S109–S122. https://doi.org/10.1086/704924

Bradley (2024) Bradley Intelligence Report The Metaverse and The Future of Business. https://www.bradley.com/insights/publications/2024/01/the-metaverse-and-the-future-of-business

Bulu ST (2012) Place presence, social presence, co-presence, and satisfaction in virtual worlds. Computers and Education 58(1). https://doi.org/10.1016/j.compedu.2011.08.024

Capatina A et al (2024) Elevating students' lives through immersive learning experiences in a safe metaverse. Int J Inf Manag 75:102723. https://doi.org/10.1016/j.ijinfomgt.2023.102723

Casey P et al (2021) Immersive virtual reality attacks and the human joystick. EEE Transactions on Dependable and Secure Computing 18(2):550–562. https://doi.org/10.1109/TDSC.2019.2907942

Choi A, Gierhart C (2022) Intellectual Property Enforcement in the Metaverse, Part 2. https://www.hklaw.com/en/insights/publications/2022/10/intellectual-property-enforcement-in-the-metaverse-part-2

Clayton J, Dyer J (2022) Roblox: The children's game with a sex problem. https://www.bbc.co.uk/news/technology-60314572

Coesel AM et al (2024) A theoretical review of the Proteus effect: understanding the underlying processes. Front Psychol 15. https://doi.org/10.3389/fpsyg.2024.1379599

Conti R, Adams M (2024) What is an NFT? Non-Fungible Tokens Explained. https://www.forbes.com/advisor/investing/cryptocurrency/nft-non-fungible-token/

Cowan K et al (2023) Can you smell the (virtual) roses? The influence of olfactory cues in virtual reality on immersion and positive brand responses. J Retail 99(3). https://doi.org/10.1016/j.jretai.2023.07.004

De Heer BA, Jones LC (2024) Tonic immobility as a defensive trauma response to rape: bridging public health and law. Violence Against Women 30(12–13):3111–3129

Decentraland (2024) Introduction. https://docs.decentraland.org/player/general/introduction/

DevX (n.d.) Head Mounted Display, https://www.devx.com/terms/head-mounted-display/

Dibbell J (1993) A Rape in Cyberspace. The Village Voice. Accessible: http://www.juliandibbell.com/texts/bungle_vv.html

Dooley K (2024) Virtual reality narratives embodied encounters in space. Springer International Publishing

Duranske D (2007) Reader Roundtable: "Virtual Rape" Claim Brings Belgian Police to Second Life. https://virtuallyblind.com/2007/04/24/open-roundtable-allegations-of-virtual-rape-bring-belgian-police-to-second-life/

Dwivedi YK et al (2023) Exploring the Darkverse: a multi-perspective analysis of the negative societal impacts of the Metaverse. Information System Fronteirs 25:2071–2114. https://doi.org/10.1007/s10796-023-10400-x

Europol (2022) Policing in the Metaverse: What Law Enforcement Needs to Know. https://www.europol.europa.eu/cms/sites/default/files/documents/Policing%20in%20the%20metaverse%20-%20what%20law%20enforcement%20needs%20to%20know.pdf

Evans L, Rzeszewski M (2020) Hermeneutic relations in VR: immersion, embodiment, presence and HCI in VR gaming. In: Fang X (ed) HCI in games. HCII 2020. Lecture notes in computer science, vol 12211. Springer, Cham. https://doi-org.ezproxy-prd.bodleian.ox.ac.uk/10.1007/978-3-030-50164-8_2

Garnham R (2017) Virtual Reality: Hype or the Future? https://www.ipsos.com/sites/default/files/ct/publication/documents/2017-10/Virtual_Reality.pdf

Goffman E (1963) Behavior in public places: notes on the social organization of gatherings. Free Press, New York

Han E, Bailenson J (2024) Social Interaction in VR, p. 3. https://doi.org/10.1093/acrefore/9780190228613.013.1489

Ibtekr (2023) Seoul Launches World's First Public Service Platform in Metaverse. https://ibtekr.org/en/cases/seoul-launches-worlds-first-public-service-platform-in-metaverse/

Interpol (2024) Metaverse: A Law Enforcement Perspective. https://www.interpol.int/en/News-and-Events/News/2024/Grooming-radicalization-and-cyber-attacks-INTERPOL-warns-of-Metacrime

Johnson A (2023) Augmented Reality (AR) Vs. Virtual Reality (VR): What's the Difference—And How Do They Work? https://www.forbes.com/sites/ariannajohnson/2023/06/02/augmented-reality-ar-vs-virtual-reality-vr-whats-the-difference-and-how-do-they-work/

Kilteni K et al (2012) The sense of embodiment in virtual reality. Presence Teleop Virt 21(4). https://doi.org/10.1162/PRES_a_00124

Knowles K (2017) What the heck is... teledildonics? https://www.forbes.com/sites/kittyknowles/2017/02/09/teledildonics-meaning-what-are-teledildonics-iot-sex-toys-vr-porn/

Knowles T (2022) Nazi sex parties hosted on children's game Roblox. https://www.thetimes.com/life-style/sex-relationships/article/nazi-sex-parties-hosted-on-childrens-game-roblox-s9vktzxx0#:~:text=The%20rooms%2C%20discovered%20in%20a,woman%20in%20a%20bondage%20outfit%E2%80%9D

Lanier J (2017) Dawn of the new everything: a journey through virtual reality. Penguin, London

Li C et al (2023) In the Metaverse Briefing Paper. p. 5. https://www3.weforum.org/docs/WEF_Interoperability_in_the_Metaverse.pdf

Malpas J (2008) The non- autonomy of the virtual: philosophical reflections on contemporary virtuality. Ubiquity - Association for Computing Machinery 2008(May):1–5. https://doi.org/10.1145/1386853.1378359

Mateu et al (2023) Jurisdiction and Enforcement Issues in the Metaverse. https://www.inta.org/wp-content/uploads/public-files/advocacy/committee-reports/20231218_JURISDICTION-AND-ENFORCEMENT-ISSUES-IN-THE-METAVERSE.pdf

McGlynn C and Rigotti C (2024) Meta-Rape: Sexual Violence, Criminal Law and the Metaverse. Accessible: https://www.claremcglynn.com/_files/ugd/e87dab_c2923fe035b24e47ac77cfd728b44f80.pdf

McKinsey & Company (2023) What is Web3? Available here: https://www.mckinsey.com/featured-insights/mckinsey-explainers/what-is-web3

Merriam-Webster (n.d.). 'Avatar', https://www.merriam-webster.com/dictionary/avatar

Meta (2021) Introducing Meta: A Social Technology Company. https://about.fb.com/news/2021/10/facebook-company-is-now-meta/

Meta (n.d.). https://about.meta.com/uk/what-is-the-metaverse/

Milani S et al (2022) Virtual reality erotica: exploring general presence, sexual presence, sexual arousal and sexual desire in women. Arch Sex Behav 51(1):565–576

Morris C (2023) The co-founder of a Canadian Private Equity Firm explains why he just acquired the internet's biggest adult entertainment site. https://fortune.com/2023/03/23/who-owns-pornhub-mindgeek-ethical-capital-canadian-private-equity-acquisition/

Mystakidis S (2022) Metaverse. Encyclopaedia 2:486–497. https://doi.org/10.3390/encyclopedia2010031

NVIDIA (2023) NVIDIA and Microsoft to Bring the Industrial Metaverse and AI to Hundreds of Millions of Enterprise Users via Azure Cloud. https://nvidianews.nvidia.com/news/nvidia-and-microsoft-to-bring-the-industrial-metaverse-and-ai-to-hundreds-of-millions-of-enterprise-users-via-azure-cloud

OWO (n.d.). https://owogame.com/sensations/

Patel NJ (2021) Reality or Fiction? https://medium.com/kabuni/fiction-vs-non-fiction-98aa0098f3b0

Peña et al (2009) The priming effects of avatars in virtual settings. Commun Res 36(6):838–856

Pierce RJ (2022) Meta's 'Safety Bubbles' Looks to Curb Virtual Harassment—But Will It Be Enough? https://www.techtimes.com/articles/271471/20220205/meta-personal-boundary-feature.htm

Rosen P (2021) A plot of digital land was just sold in the metaverse for $2.43 million—more than most homes in NYC and San Francisco cost. Accessible: https://markets.businessinsider.com/news/currencies/metaverse-property-decentraland-sale-price-mana-coin-cryptocurrency-2021-11

Rzeszewski et al (2024) Interviewing in the metaverse: the renewed importance of location and embodiment. Appl Geogr 167:103295. https://doi.org/10.1016/j.apgeog.2024.103295

Sales N (2024) A girl was allegedly raped in the metaverse. Is this the beginning of a dark new future? https://www.theguardian.com/commentisfree/2024/jan/05/metaverse-sexual-assault-vr-game-online-safety-meta

Schott D (2017) 'World of Warcraft' Has a Rape Problem. https://www.vice.com/en/article/world-of-warcraft-has-a-rape-problem/?utm_source=mbtwitter

Slater M (1999) Measuring presence: a response to the Witmer and singer presence questionnaire. Presence Teleop Virt 8(5). https://doi.org/10.1162/105474699566477

Stephenson N (1992) Snow crash. Bantam Books, New York

Tabahriti S (2022) Meta is putting a stop to virtual groping in its metaverse by creating safety bubbles around avatars. https://www.businessinsider.com/meta-metaverse-virtual-groping-personal-boundary-safety-bubble-horizons-venues-2022-2

Tsukayama H (2018) Roblox, an online kids game, explains how a hack allowed a character's virtual rape. https://www.washingtonpost.com/technology/2018/07/17/roblox-an-online-kids-game-explains-how-hack-allowed-characters-virtual-rape/

Valente J (2024) Governing the Metaverse. University of Cincinnati Intellectual Property and Computer Law Journal 9(2):135–149

Vanian J (2024) Meta's Reality Labs posts $4.5 billion loss in second quarter. https://www.cnbc.com/2024/07/31/metas-reality-labs-posts-4point5-billion-loss-in-second-quarter.html

Virtual Reality Society (n.d.), 'Head Mounted Displays (HMDs)', https://www.vrs.org.uk/virtual-reality-gear/head-mounted-displays/

West T (2024) The Power of Touch, Exploring Haptic Technology in Modern Branding. https://juicebox.co.id/haptic-technology-modern-branding/

Wiederhold B (2023) Haptics: making the Metaverse a touching experience. Cyberpsychol Behav Soc Netw 26(9):668–669. https://doi.org/10.1089/cyber.2023.29278.editorial

WIPO (n.d.) H2L: Bridging the Gap Between Humans, Machines and Virtual Environments. https://www.wipo.int/wipo_magazine/en/ip-at-work/2023/h2l.html

Yee N, Bailenson J (2007) The Proteus effect: the effect of transformed self-representation on behaviour. Hum Commun Res 33(3):271–290. https://doi.org/10.1111/j.1468-2958.2007.00299.x

Zhang J (2023) Free Movement of Virtual Goods in the Metaverse: Is the Construction of the Metaverse legally possible under EU Copyright Law? Trinity College Dublin Legal Studies Research Paper Series 19/2023

Chapter 3
The Sexual Offences Act 2003 in a Virtual Future: Some Key Issues

3.1 Introduction

The Sexual Offences Act 2003 begins with sections on the four principal sexual offences recognised in English and Welsh law.[1]

These are:

1. Rape
2. Assault by Penetration
3. Sexual Assault
4. Causing a Person to Engage in Sexual Activity Without Consent[2]

These are the four offences that this book will primarily focus on, alongside the statutory definitions of consent and their attaching presumptions of s.74–76 of the Act and the statutory definition of 'sexual' at s.78.

However, before such discussions, the remainder of this chapter is dedicated to three essential points. The first is the identification of the actor: it is important to distinguish the controller of the avatar and the avatar itself. The second pertains to the identification of the 'act' in virtual reality. I will argue that individuals can, and regularly do, perform actions in virtual reality and that these actions can form the basis of a criminal offence. This chapter will then conclude with a short discussion of the wrong at the core of sexual offences.

[1] See Temkin and Ashworth (2004) on the distinction between these offences and the impact of their introduction in the SOA 2003.

[2] Sexual Offences Act 2003 s.4.

R. Procktor, *The Sexual Offences Act 2003 and Virtual Reality*, SpringerBriefs in Law, https://doi.org/10.1007/978-3-032-10397-0_3

3.2 The Actor

Who should the criminal law identify as the actor: the avatar or the individual controlling it? This section will argue that the actors that the criminal law should concern themselves with are the individuals controlling the avatars rather than exclusively the avatars themselves.

This is important for two reasons. Firstly, as avatars are the mere icons or representations that individuals are represented by or, as in the case of the metaverse, embodied in, they are not agents in their own right. It is the operator of the avatar which controls its movement. Secondly, this is important as not all avatars are controlled by humans. Non-playable characters (NPCs)[3] are often nowadays operated by artificial intelligence (AI). For example, chatbots have already been placed in VR games, responding to users spontaneously using machine learning.[4]

The legal situation of the NPC and the user-operated avatar should be further distinguished. The NPC has no autonomous control over what it does. Contrastingly, the user-operated avatar is responsive to the specific deployment of the user. Moving your arm causes the avatar's arm to move (the intended outcome), just as moving your hand to change gears in the car causes the gear change.

In his discussion of virtual sexual assault, Danaher provides a useful classification for determining whether interactions between avatars ought to incur criminal liability.[5] Only certain factual scenarios ought to interest the criminal law. I agree with Danaher that any scenarios which involve NPCs ought not to fall under the SOA.[6] Equally, although the potential output may be cause for concern, individuals who create NPC AI girlfriends unable to say no or programmed to physically resist

[3] An NPC is a character in a game not controlled by players.

[4] For this in action, see: Gingas (2024) 'YOU can FEEL PAIN in SKYRIM VR—Episode 3' [Video] https://www.youtube.com/watch?v=lHc-oQrkEH4.

[5] Danaher (2018), p. 8:

1. Human user—virtual character
2. Perpetrator—victim
3. Text-based—Immersive

Danaher labels this final distinction as: avatar-immersive. He distinguishes avatar-interactions as "text based interactions via avatars" or "visual interactions in Second Life" and immersive interactions, where "actions performed via the virtual representations are immediately transduced into effects on real human bodies: the users can feel completely psychologically immersed in the experience.", p. 7. I fail to see the meaningful distinction between 'virtual representations' and 'avatars'. The notion of avatars is central to literature on VR and immersive technologies: see Freeman et al. (2020) and Freeman and Acena (2022). Although this may appear a semantic point, it is important to consider in the way that we perceive the avatar moving forward. Therefore, I prefer the terminology "text-based" and "immersive".

[6] *Ibid.*

sexual advances before submitting to being overpowered should not fall within the s.1–4 of the SOA either.[7]

What about virtually controlled avatars attacking human-controlled ones? Here, there is no issue in identifying the victim but rather more in identifying the defendant. The question as to whether a company could be a named defendant in a case charged under the SOA 2003 seems counter-intuitive, especially as the statute currently specifies that "a person", in the singular, "commits an offence" under the SOA 2003. Whether this "person" could be extended to include a legal person remains untested. In addition, it is difficult to prove any intent to fulfil the mens rea of the offence on behalf of AI-operated avatars, therefore the case appears closer to a product liability matter than a criminal one. It does, however, raise an interesting question: could a legal person be a defendant in a sexual offences criminal case? If so, is there an effective sanction, given the practical difficulty of incarceration? Fines against major companies have already been criticised as ineffective, partly because they are seen as "just part of the cost of doing business."[8] This is undesirable considering the severity of sexual offences.

In short, the only type of interaction which ought to currently concern criminal law is between human users as perpetrators and victims. This may be dealt with in different ways depending on the level of immersion. For example, a text-based world is likely to lend itself to a communication offence, whereas an immersive world is better dealt with under the heads of the four primary sexual offences.

3.3 Distinguishing Actions, Actors and Avatars

Let us return for a minute to Mr. Bungle.[9] Following the incident, it was later revealed that Mr. Bungle and his subsequent manifestations were not one person at all but the communal property of a floor of a dorm at New York University.[10] In this medium, where individuals take on roles and communicate through text, it is difficult to identify the criminal act: student A may have typed one thing, student B may have amended it, and student C may have pressed send. Unless we can identify a precise message or point in time at which their victim developed PTSD, it is going to be difficult to ascribe liability for any crime, lest not for rape.[11]

[7] This is not to say that they should not potentially be the subject of some form of communications offence. For example, where the avatar is a deepfake of a known person, and particularly if the avatar is represented as a child, there may be good reason why the law should criminalise such behavior. However, considering that the law should be focused on bodily and sexual autonomy, chatbot-operated avatars have no such autonomy and therefore should be excluded.

[8] Espinoza (2023).

[9] Dibbell (1993), see the previous chapter for a discussion of this event.

[10] *Ibid.*

[11] That is at least on an individual basis. There may be some form of accessorial or joint liability.

However, there is a distinction between the text-based examples of the past, as was the case with Mr. Bungle, and the current issues faced in the metaverse. Mr. Bungle used words: there was never any suggestion of contact or threat of sexual violence offline. Equally, although traumatic and violating, the situation appears closer to the line of case law from *Chan-Fook*[12] to *Ireland*[13] regarding offences against the person and psychiatric injury: if the victim did go on to develop PTSD, there may be an actionable claim under the Offences Against the Person Act 1861, or potentially under the head of sexual harassment. It is, however, unlikely to be rape.

However, the metaverse is not a space in which *exclusively* pixelated avatars or typed sentences interact. Instead, it is a space where avatars are the vehicles through which individuals exercise their agency and can meaningfully 'act' through them in the context of a wider community, often with physical repercussions.

One of the main barriers to imposing liability for acts in virtual reality is the assumption that interactions between avatars are pixelated and, to put it bluntly, not real. Therefore, the first hurdle is proving that the interaction between individuals in avatar form can fulfil this "physicality requirement" in a way that is more than merely illusory or tokenistic. This requires confronting the often-intuitive assumption that interactions between avatars are merely pixels in a digital space.

3.3.1 *Why Criminalise Acts?*

There are two main types of reasons for requiring an 'act' as an element of a criminal offence: descriptive reasons and normative reasons.[14]

Descriptively, the 'act' requirement is a useful one in identifying the structural aspects of the law: what is the conduct that the law seeks to punish? Normatively, it acts as a double-edged sword, providing both reasons for imposing criminal liability and protection from criminal prosecution unless it can be proven.[15] This strengthens its "intuitive plausibility", which largely derives from the types of conduct that it excludes from liability: thoughts or fantasies of criminal wrongdoing and involuntary body movements.[16]

---

[12] [1994] 1 WLR 689.

[13] [1997] UKHL 34: words spoken over the telephone can constitute an act under Offences Against the Person Act.

[14] Duff (2004), p. 70.

[15] Notwithstanding any attempt offences that may arise in the preparation of the act. However, this preparation is an act, even if not the final intended act.

[16] Supra (Duff 2004); note also that this is not uncontested within the realm of philosophy. See further, Child (2020).

3.3.2 The "It's Not Real" Objection

The first objection levelled at identifying acts in virtual reality is the objection that the actions are not real. However, it is artificial to ignore the impact that interaction online has on our non-virtual lives: intravirtual actions often have extravirtual consequences.[17]

For example, words written in an email have no less legal significance than words written by hand: both may convey a change in employment status or be the focus of a defamation claim. Equally, sexual interaction that occurs through a digital medium can still be the target of criminal law. Crimes added to the SOA 2003 since its inception concerning the commission of sexual offences online have primarily fallen under the broader heading of communications offences. For example, the new cyber-flashing[18] and image-based sexual abuse[19] offences inserted into the SOA by the Online Safety Act in December 2023 are both communications offences. The 'act' identifiable here is found in the non-consensual creation and dissemination of sexual content. However, it would be artificial to hold in this situation that the tapping of a keyboard and clicking of a mouse was the criminal act itself. It was the accessing of the websites or the uploading of the photos. The actions in the non-virtual (the clicking of the mouse or the tapping of the keyboard) facilitate the crime which occurs in the virtual. However, the harm is not merely limited intravirtually but manifests extravirtually. These are not just pixels or lines of code. There is no automatic reason why conduct in the metaverse ought to be subjected to an exclusion from "reality" on the basis that human conduct is facilitated through technology.

This relates to the second interesting point that the objection of 'it's not real' fails to address: the dependence of the virtual world on the non-virtual one.[20] Actions cannot simply be isolated online—they trigger a chain of events in the non-virtual, even if the primary manifestation of those acts is in the virtual world. On a very broad reading, the action still has its roots in the non-virtual world. This is true irrespective of the use of haptic technology. However, this does not mean that *all* actions manifest in the same way. For example, consider one of the comments which followed the announcement of the British Police investigation into the rape of a sixteen-year-old in the metaverse: "I was killed in Call of Duty, been waiting for my killers to be brought to justice." There is a simple response to such knee-jerk objections. Avatars are not alive and thus incapable of being killed. Therefore, the "death" of an avatar is a virtual action which does not manifest extravirtually: being killed

---

[17] Using the words of Danaher (2018) here, cited from Brey (2003). Intra virtual is when the actions impact only the virtual representations. Extra virtual actions occur when the actions equally impact the controller/individual in the non-virtual world.

[18] S.66A Sexual Offences Act, as inserted by s. 187 Online Safety Act 2023.

[19] S. 66B Sexual Offences Act, as inserted by s. 188 Online Safety Act 2023. Often referred to in popular media as 'revenge porn.'

[20] For a broader discussion on this, see Danaher (2022), pp. 266–268.

in Call of Duty does not kill the user.[21] In the same way, avatars distinct from human users cannot be sexually assaulted. However, in cases such as Nina Jane Patel's,[22] the effects can manifest extravirtually: the user, not the avatar, has suffered the wrong.[23]

The specific *actus reus* of the different sexual offences will be discussed in the following chapter, but it suffices at this point to suggest that there are compelling reasons why we should again lean into the flexibility of the common law and consider some acts in the metaverse to be capable of incurring criminal liability. There are compelling reasons to resist the objection of 'it's not real.'

3.4 Sexual Offences and Autonomy

A detailed analysis of the precise theoretical basis for sexual offences is beyond the scope of this book. It suffices to note that autonomy is a broad term already used by the courts and by the government as a conceptual basis, contrasting with a prior focus on 'force-based models' of sexual offences.[24] Autonomy is taken here in this broad sense, however, as much of this book focuses on situating novel forms of sexual offence within their broader social context, it draws on a relational account of autonomy.[25] It is useful, however, to provide an overview and to outline some of the key tensions in the current academic debate.

Sexual offences originally emerged as property offences aimed at repairing the damage done to the social and economic value of the damaged commodity: a woman.[26] For centuries, penetration provided an easily identifiable actus reus of the offence of rape. Equally, contextualising the offence, it makes sense that penetration, the actual physical destruction of the economic value of a woman, would be that identifying marker. The 'property' of present and future male family members had been infringed upon, and such infringement constituted a crime.

In this context, if we take rape as a proprietary offence, penetration seems a fair starting point. However, rape is no longer a property offence. Instead, both domestic and international legal systems are starting to view rape as a violation of autonomy.[27] Writing from a philosophical perspective, Gardner and Shute pose the idea of

[21] It may still manifest extravirtually, for example, as a violation of bodily integrity if haptic technology is worn and being 'shot' causes vibrations on the body. For a discussion of this, see Chap. 6.

[22] Set out in Chap. 3.

[23] This is premised on an account of the wrong of rape which centers on V's sexual autonomy, discussed in more detail in the following section.

[24] On the force-based vs consent-based distinction, see Zuloaga (2023), esp. pp. 158–160.

[25] See for explanation: Herring (2009).

[26] Brundage (1987), p. 48. See the original texts Brundage refers to at Dig. 47. 10. 9. 4 (Ulpian); Cod. 9. 20. 1 (Antoninus Pius).

[27] MC v. Bulgaria, App. No. 39272/98, European Court of Human Rights, Judgment of 4 December 2003, esp. at [164]–[166]; Prosecutor v. Jean-Paul Akayesu, ICTR-96-4-T, International Criminal

a 'pure case' of rape, where a victim has no memory of the assault and no physical pain as a result of the rape.[28] They suggest, and rightly so, that this is still a serious violation and criminal wrong.

Herring, writing about opponents of the view that rape is a violation of autonomy, notes that:

> [they] argue that regarding rape as essentially an interference with autonomy neglects the physicality of rape. There is an invasion of the body, and not just with the incorporeal notion of autonomy. What [Gardner and Shute] use as their paradigm of rape appears to bear little connection with the reality of most rape cases.[29]

It is accepted that the pure case bears very little connection with the reality of most cases that are legally classified as rape. However, Gardner and Shute's argument still applies to a range of sexual offences. Looking at the broader picture, a purely physical perspective tells us little about *why* society should criminalise sexual offences. If the identifying feature of rape is a physical intrusion without consent, nothing more, then what is the fair labelling justification for distinguishing between offences against the person and sexual offences? Equally, as already discussed, the narrow notion of physicality as dependent on penetration present in the current law is inadequate considering the realism and capability of technology already present on the market, let alone those still in development.

Another criticism is that overreliance on incorporeal notions such as autonomy would result in an offence defined primarily by its victims or as an over-prescriptive conception of autonomy.[30] Such views will be tested in later chapters. Other scholars have reconceptualised autonomy as integrity[31] or view sexual offences as an inevitable consequence of patriarchy.[32] Autonomy is, in itself, a contested term capable of holding a range of meanings.[33] Another option is to view sexual autonomy as linked to sexual integrity, encompassing the absolute negative right to refuse sexual activity and the positive right to choose to engage in sexual activity.[34]

Again, this book does not take a definitive perspective on the precise wrong underpinning sexual offences. It will refer to autonomy in a broad sense across the course of its discussion as this is a key element in both statutory drafting and academic writing, considering at times how different conceptions of autonomy may impact how the law should be applied or ought to be developed.[35]

Tribunal for Rwanda, Judgment, 2 September 1998; Munro (2008); Wegerstadt (2021), p. 12 using the language of 'sexual self-determination'.

[28] Gardner and Shute (2000).

[29] Herring (2022), p. 109.

[30] Rubenfeld (2013).

[31] Lacey (1998)

[32] Mackinnon (2016).

[33] Feinberg (1989), Ch. 12.

[34] Gibson (2020) takes a similar position.

[35] In particular, this is evident in the discussion in Chapter Four involving consent.

3.5 Conclusion

This chapter has outlined some of the key issues requiring consideration at the outset of an inquiry into sexual offences in the metaverse. It has argued that there are compelling theoretical reasons to discount the common objection that actions in the metaverse are not real and that there is a logical way to identify the actors in these crimes. Finally, although noting the ambiguity surrounding the term 'autonomy', it concludes by noting that considerations surrounding dignity and autonomy are becoming increasingly central in discussions surrounding sexual offences. The arguments in the following chapters will be situated against this background.

References

Brey P (2003) The social ontology of virtual environments. Am J Econ Sociol 62(1):269–282
Brundage J (1987) Law, sex and Christian Society in medieval Europe. University of Chicago Press, Chicago
Child J (2020) Defence of a basic voluntary act requirement in criminal law from philosophies of action. New Criminal Law Rev 23(4):437–470. https://doi.org/10.1525/nclr.2020.23.4.437
Danaher J (2018) The law and ethics of virtual sexual assault. In: Barflied W, Blitz M (eds) Research handbook on the law of virtual and augmented reality. Edward Elgar Publishers, Cheltenham, p 12
Danaher J (2022) The ethics of virtual sexual assault. In: Véliz C (ed) The Oxford handbook of digital ethics. Oxford University Press, Oxford
Dibbell J (1993) A Rape in Cyberspace, The Village Voice
Duff A (2004) Action, the act requirement and criminal liability. Royal Institute Philos Supplements 55:69–103. https://doi.org/10.1017/S135824610000864X
Espinoza J (2023) Why BigTech Fines do not Work. https://www.ft.com/content/ba6eb664-b981-42d7-b24a-65e7e19889f8
Feinberg J (1989) The moral limits of the criminal law. Vol 3. Ch.12. Oxford University Press, Oxford
Freeman G, Acena D (2022) Acting out queer identity: embodied visibility in social VR. Proc ACM Human-Computer Interaction 6(CSCW2) Article 263:1–32. https://doi.org/10.1145/3555153
Freeman G et al (2020) My body, My Avatar: how people perceive their avatars in virtual reality. In: CHI EA '20 Conference on Human Factors in Computing Systems. pp. 1–8. doi: https://doi.org/10.1145/3334480.3382923
Gardner J, Shute S (2000) The wrongness of rape. In: Horder J (ed) Oxford essays in jurisprudence, fourth series, pp 193–218
Gibson M (2020) Deceptive sexual relations: a theory of criminal liability. Oxf J Leg Stud 40(1):82–109
Gingas VR (2024) 'YOU can FEEL PAIN in SKYRIM VR—Episode 3' [Video]. https://www.youtube.com/watch?v=lHc-oQrkEH4
Herring J (2009) Relational autonomy and rape. In: Day Sclater S et al (eds) Regulating autonomy: sex, reproduction and family. Bloomsbury Publishing, London. Ch.4
Herring J (2022) Great debates in criminal law. Bloomsbury Publishing, London
Lacey N (1998) Unspeakable subjects, impossible rights: sexuality, integrity and criminal law. Can J Law Jurisprudence 11(1):47–68
Mackinnon C (2016) Rape redefined. Harv Law Policy Rev 10(2):431–477

Munro V (2008) Constructing consent: legislating freedom and legitimating constraint in the expression of sexual autonomy. Akron Law Rev 41(5):923–955
Rubenfeld J (2013) The riddle of rape-by-deception and the myth of sexual autonomy. Yale Law J 122(6):1372–1443
Temkin J, Ashworth A (2004) The sexual offences act 2003: (1) rape, sexual assaults and the problems of consent. Criminal Law Rev:328–334
Wegerstadt L (2021) Theorising sexual harassment and criminalization in a Swedish context. Bergen J Criminal Law Criminal Justice 9(2):61–81. https://doi.org/10.15845/bjclcj.v9i2.3525
Zuloaga P (2023) Unlearning agreement: imagining the law without consent. In: James-Hawkins L, Ryan-Flood R (eds) Consent: gender, power and subjectivity. Routledge, Abingdon, pp 153–168

Chapter 4
Penetration and Physicality

4.1 Introduction

When the Belgian police announced that they were beginning an investigation into a rape that occurred in Second Life in 2006, scepticism was rife.[1] The main concerns about assimilating sexual offences in Second Life with the 'real life' crime of rape were vividly summed up in a 2007 Wired article: "No matter how disturbed you are by a brutal sexual attack online, you cannot equate it to shivering in the hospital with an assailants sweat or other excretions still damp on your body."[2] It is the perceived lack of physicality in virtual reality that gives rise to the greatest amount of scepticism for prosecuting rape and other sexual offences in the metaverse under the 2003 Act.

To be clear, I will not make the argument that the current law could be widely used to prosecute rape in the metaverse. Under the narrow approach taken by the 2003 Act, save for the use of some specific technologies, sexual interaction in the metaverse cannot fulfil the requirement of penetration. As regards sexual assault, it will be argued that this is currently possible in the metaverse with the use of haptic technologies. However, I will argue, perhaps more controversially, that the current law is underinclusive and excessively phallocentric, especially considering the increasingly different ways that sexual interaction is experienced. These considerations are rooted in an analysis of how sexual interaction in the metaverse fundamentally challenges some of the enduring assumptions entrenched in the 2003 Act and attempts to shine a light on why, a mere 20 years after its inception, the SOA already appears to lag behind lived experience. As a result, it will suggest one way in which we may want to reform the SOA 2003 to better accommodate the diverse reality of sexual interaction in modern society.

[1] Duranske (2007).

[2] Lynn (2007).

R. Procktor, *The Sexual Offences Act 2003 and Virtual Reality*, SpringerBriefs in Law, https://doi.org/10.1007/978-3-032-10397-0_4

4.2 Applying the Sexual Offences Act 2003

Although much discussion has focused on the possibility of rape in the metaverse, there are fewer conversations surrounding the possibility of other sexual offences, in particular sexual assault. Considering that this is likely to be the predominant form of unwanted sexual interaction in the metaverse, it merits further attention.

The present section will explore the applicability of the current s.1–4 SOA 2003. Building on this analysis, the following section will then posit one method of accommodating sexual interaction in VR through a revised framework of the SOA or the addition of another section in the statute.

4.2.1 Sexual Assault

The current s.3 of the SOA 2003 makes it an offence for a person to (a) intentionally touch another person, (B) (b) that touching is sexual, (c) B does not consent to the touching, and (d) A does not reasonably believe that B consents.[3]

The primary difficulty in the metaverse context is proving that there has been 'intentional touching'. What is seen as "touching" in the non-virtual is often assessed intuitively. However, in the era of technology, this has begun to be put under scrutiny. For an analysis of what the criminal law has viewed as 'touching' in the past, it is useful to refer to case law stemming from the Offences Against the Person Act 1861.

It is well established that even the slightest touch can constitute a battery: touching someone's hair,[4] throwing a bucket of water at another person,[5] or touching someone's clothes[6] may all give rise to criminal liability. Therefore, even without haptic sensors designed to cause pain or the infliction of any harm resulting in a recognised medical condition, the vibrations produced should be sufficient to constitute battery if they were not consented to and the touching was sexual.[7]

One objection would be that there is no direct body-to-body contact in the case of interactions in the metaverse. This fails.

Take, for example, *Fagan*.[8] Here, F was convicted of assaulting a police officer. He had been reversing his car into a parking spot, directed by a policeman, and when asked to park closer to the curb, drove onto the policeman's foot. He refused to move the car even after several calls from the policeman. He was convicted of

[3] S.3 Sexual Offences Act 2003.

[4] *DPP v Smith* [2006] EWHC 94 (Admin).

[5] *Pursell v Horn* [1838] 112 ER 966.

[6] *R v Thomas* [1985] 81 Cr App R 331.

[7] By sexual, reference could still be made to s.78 SOA 2003. Sexual touching is construed objectively; for a recent analysis of this provision, see *R v Kennedy* [2024] SAC Crim 8.

[8] *Fagan v MPP* [1969] 1 QB 439.

assault by the first instance court but appealed on the basis that the act of the mounting of the wheel onto the foot could not be assault as there had been no body-to-body contact.[9] The Court of Appeal dismissed this argument, concluding that:

> where an assault involves a battery, it matters not, in our judgement, whether the battery is inflicted directly by the body of the offender, or *through the medium of some weapon or instrument controlled by the action of the offender.* An assault may be committed by the laying of a hand upon another, and the action does not cease to be an assault if it is a stick held in the hand and not the hand itself which is laid on the person of the victim.[10]

Consider then *DPP v K (a minor).*[11] K left his chemistry lesson with a vial of acid, intending to test it on a piece of toilet paper in the school bathrooms. Whilst there, he was interrupted and poured the vial of sulphuric acid into the hand dryer to avoid detection. The next student to use the hand dryer suffered chemical burns and K was prosecuted under s.47 of the OAPA. K never directly touched V. K did not even throw the vial of acid itself onto V. Yet, the AR requirement was still fulfilled, even in the absence of a direct physical connection.[12]

If we place these interactions in the context of the metaverse, there should be little issue with A causing the haptic sensors on B's body to be activated and that this could constitute battery and is, therefore, possible for "touching" to occur. If this touching is applied sexually, the crime would fall under this section.

However, there is an inconsistent outcome if the current law is applied unchanged. As a result of the touching requirement, individuals who are not wearing haptic technology will not be protected, or at least only be protected on a lesser level. For example, in a game where the "haptic status"[13] of a user is displayed, perpetrators may deliberately target those without haptic technologies to fall under the lesser crime if caught. Irrespective of any displayed status, the sentence that a defendant should receive should not be contingent on whether they happened to attack an individual with or without haptic technology.[14]

Additionally, the sense of "being there" often obscures the impossibility of physical contact, even if momentarily, in the face of a potential threat. Given the experience of the metaverse as immersed, embodied and present, it will still be difficult for the victim to distinguish between the virtual and the non-virtual. In a comical example of this difficulty distinguishing between the virtual and non-virtual, one man found himself the star of a viral video after he "face-plant[ed] on flat ground as his

---

[9] Note however that there was another aspect of the appeal relating to the coexistence of the actus reus and mens rea.

[10] Supra (n9), p.444 at E-G, Emphasis added.

[11] [*1990*] 1 WLR 1067.

[12] See also on this point, *Haystead v Chief Constable of Derbyshire* [2000] 3 All ER 89.

[13] A hypothetical signal visible to other players to inform them whether the user is wearing haptic technology.

[14] There is an argument, that I am grateful to Moayad Karar for pointing out, that this kind of moral luck is rife within the criminal law. This is partially addressed later on in the chapter, in the argument for distinguishing sexual assault and sexual battery.

avatar [tumbled] from a cliff."[15] Therefore, whilst some cases may be able to be prosecuted under s.3, the current exclusive focus on physicality leaves a lot to be desired, leaving individuals like Patel without protection.

4.2.2 Rape and Assault by Penetration

I have grouped these two offences as, under the current law, they can both be dealt with quite summarily. Rape, currently requiring penile penetration of person B by person A, is currently impossible in the metaverse. It will very likely remain so.

Assault by penetration under s.2 is a different matter but would require a very specific factual circumstance to be prosecuted. Take the situation of a virtual cam-girl using technology similar to VexRuby.[16] Here, it may be possible for interactive penetrative sex toys to be used within the context of a paid session. Were the cam girl to use a safe word, asking the controller of the toy to stop the penetrative act, and they refused, this may come under the protection of the current s.2: there is intentional penetration of the body with an object, and there is no reasonable belief that B consents. There would still be barriers to overcome in reaching this conclusion. For example, A was not present in the room at the time of the assault. There was no physical contact between the object and the perpetrator. However, it may be suggested that the statute does not require contact but 'intentional penetration.' This could be feasibly extended to a situation where A is not present but retains control of the operation of the object penetrating B and refuses to stop when asked.

4.2.3 Causing a Person to Engage in Sexual Activity

The case of the meta-cam girl may be closer to the line of cases under s.4 SOA 2003: causing a person to engage in sexual activity without consent. Section 4 has been often overlooked in research and national statistics.[17] It represents two possible offences: one requiring penetration and one which does not.[18] Section 4 is broad, covering a range of different situations from forced masturbation[19] to forced-to-penetrate cases.[20]

This is a possible approach but is still riddled with complexities. The perpetrator is not forcing any behaviour from the victim, threatening them to masturbate or to

[15] HAL 90210 (2016).

[16] See Chap. 2.

[17] Weare (2020), p. 2.

[18] SOA 2003, s .4 (5).

[19] *R v Devonald* [2008] EWCA Crim 52.

[20] For an in-depth analysis of forced to penetrate cases, see Weare and Hulley (2019).

interact with anyone else. The perpetrator is in control and responsible for the movement of the penetrative sex toy. This appears to be different to the type of offence that s.4 is intended to cover. For example, the victim in *R v Devonald* is likely to have the same recourse through the SOA if the interaction happened in the metaverse as they did when it occurred during a video call. Therefore, the offence under s.4 could be used exceptionally broadly in the metaverse. However, there is a question as to how far a victim could be said to have "engaged" in such activity. In the example given by Patel in the first section of this chapter, it seems artificial to say that there was any real *engagement* in the sexual activity forced on them. From the Setting the Boundaries paper, it certainly seems as if this was the distinction that the Home Office had in mind:

> 2.20.1. One aspect of sexual behaviour which is potentially very serious, and clearly criminal, is that of compelling others to carry out sexual acts against their will. It is possible, for example, for someone to force another person to perform a sexual act on themselves, the compellor or a third party. That act is not voluntary – it may indeed be a criminal act such as sexual assault or even rape or sexual assault by penetration…"[21]

Section 4 is then not about infliction *per se*, but about compulsion. It is uncomfortable to hold that individuals subjected to unwanted sexual acts in the metaverse have somehow been a participant in the acts done to them, whereas in the non-virtual world their role would be viewed differently. Without a reformulation of substance and understanding of s.4, it remains an undesirable basis for the criminalisation of unwanted sexual activity in the metaverse.

If we were to invoke it, the same reliance on specialised technologies such as teledildonics exists for the penetrative offences under s.4. However, the non-penetrative offences are still largely unaccommodated within the criminal law.

4.2.4 Concluding Remarks

Overall, the SOA 2003 is currently incapable of accommodating the wide variety of sexual offences which are possible in the metaverse. The technology is new and evolving, creating a new lens through which to evaluate the law. Currently, victims of sexual offences in the metaverse will likely only have a claim if they are wearing haptic technology, despite the persistence of invasive and intense feelings of violation due to unwanted sexual interaction. The law needs to develop to accommodate the multitude of ways that technology can, is, and will be used to perpetrate degrading and violative assaults. The remainder of this chapter is an attempt to conceptualise how it might do so.

[21] Home Office (2000), para 2.20.1.

4.3 A New Approach?

There are three ways that sexual interaction in virtual reality could be addressed by criminal law.

The first is to charge each crime as an attempted sexual offence. There is some merit to this. However, such an approach could be an affront to the victim, invalidating their experience and suggesting that the offence itself was never actually carried out.

Both other alternatives involve statutory changes. The first would be to create a separate statute or a section within the SOA 2003 dealing with meta-sexual offences.[22] The second would be to amend s.1–4 of the SOA 2003 itself. I suspect that there would be rather more push-back to the latter due to the range of effects that this could have on the non-virtual set of offences. It may also be pertinent to start with the introduction of a "meta-sexual offences" section rather than a complete overhaul to allow time to see precisely how the technology evolves. This is true, but it ought also to be noted that there are aspects of the current law an analysis of potential 'meta-sexual offences' highlights as inadequate. We may still need to change aspects of s.1–4, even if not replacing them entirely, to ensure coherence.

The potential approaches and offences that will be discussed are:

1. Intimate Intrusions
2. Sexual Assault (including Sexual Assault and Sexual Battery)
3. Causing a person to engage in sexual activity without consent
4. Procurement of Sexual Activity by Deception (or some other related deception offence)
5. Rape by Penetration
6. Constructive Rape

These will now be examined in turn.[23]

4.3.1 *Intimate Intrusions*

In a recent article, McGlynn set out a proposal for a new form of sexual offence: an offence of intimate intrusions.[24] McGlynn proposes an offence which can adapt flexibly, encompassing the "wide-ranging, ever-changing, violating" conduct

[22] I use the word meta in relation to McGlynn's definition and discussion of language in 'meta-rape': McGlynn and Rigotti (2024).

[23] This section will be written as if the proposal were to completely change s.1–4 rather than introduce a new section for 'meta-sexual offences'. This is primarily to tease out some of the tensions that may arise if this approach is taken. However, the same proposals could be followed without a complete rewrite of the principal sexual offences, instead titled 'meta-sexual assault', 'meta-sexual battery' etc.

[24] McGlynn (2024).

experienced by women, which is "*sufficiently harmful and unacceptable to constitute criminal wrongdoing.*"[25]

Aimed at ensuring that the lived experiences of women subjected to sexual harm and abuse were placed in the foreground of discussion, 'intimate intrusion' functions as "an umbrella term which describes and conceptualises the range of women's experiences of harm and abuse."[26] Notably, such a term defies the conventional categorisation of criminal law, ensuring that the infinite number of ways that women are violated is subject to criminal law without the need to provide distinct and often exclusionary categories.[27]

The proposed offence is intended to operate as a blanket protection for accommodating women's experiences where they fall outside the conventional categories of criminal law. Such an argument conceptualises sexual violence as a 'continuum' rather than a smattering of singular offences, allowing for greater flexibility and understanding of women's experiences.[28]

McGlynn's analysis is particularly concerned with communications offences and production offences, such as the production of deepfake pornography or forms of cyberflashing. Given the immersed, present and embodied nature of the metaverse, sexual activity in VR seems markedly different to such offences, even though they are both rooted in violations of an individual's sexual autonomy and dignity. Therefore, we should be careful to distinguish an approach which facilitates an understanding of criminal law beyond the limits of rigid categorisation from an approach dispensing with categorisation altogether. There are good normative reasons for maintaining groupings of factual situations, from both a fair-labelling standpoint and because they improve public understanding of what specific behaviour constitutes criminal activity. Therefore, whilst this chapter maintains that all sexual offences are a form of intimate intrusion, they are so in different ways. In the interests of fair labelling and clarity, we ought to delineate where we can. However, it ought to be noted that this can still eschew a hierarchical structure. Instead, we ought to look at the law against a canvas of intimate intrusions, with groupings of different kinds of conduct to allow like cases to be considered alike and provide some structure and clarity.

The proposed framework can be summed up as follows:

1. All sexual offences are a form of intimate intrusion.
2. Intrusions can be of different practical types.
3. We ought to group types of intrusion as separate offences against the canvas of intimate intrusions more broadly.
4. Such an approach would allow the law to be flexible, accommodating novel forms of sexual violation and abuse whilst maintaining clarity.

---

[25] *Ibid.* p. 207.

[26] *Ibid.* p. 195.

[27] *Ibid.*

[28] *Ibid.*

Therefore, conceptualising intimate intrusions as the background against which we can understand sexual offences allows both flexibility within the law and a way for victims to be able to situate themselves within the broader context of sexual offences, recognising the blurred lines between different categories.

4.3.2 Sexual Assault (Including Sexual Assault and Sexual Battery)

The proposed offences of sexual assault and sexual battery would replace the current s.3 of the SOA 2003. Similar to its non-sexual counterparts in the common law, the offences would distinguish between situations of physical contact and the absence of physical contact. In the context of VR, this distinction is largely relevant in the context of distinguishing situations involving haptic technologies and those not involving haptic technologies.

Sexual battery would be defined in the same way as the current provision on sexual assault: it is an offence for a person to intentionally touch another person sexually without their consent. Sexual assault could be defined as "an act by which a person intentionally causes another to apprehend immediate unwanted touching of a sexual nature."

The first part is deliberately identical to the understanding of assault of the common law, primarily for practical reasons. Chiefly, it provides a legal foundation to begin to assess the situation and greater clarity in identifying potential criminal acts.

Concerning the apprehension and immediacy requirements, remembering that existence in VR is immersed, embodied, and present,[29] it can be difficult to distinguish between outcomes of actions in the virtual and non-virtual. Therefore, this is unlikely to pose an insurmountable problem in the metaverse.

4.3.2.1 Distinguishing Sexual Assault and Sexual Battery

Again, for pragmatic reasons, the proposed offences would mirror the division present in the Offences Against the Person Act 1861. This begs the question: why distinguish them from their non-sexual counterparts in the first place? Interestingly, sexual offences first found statutory footing in the 1861 Act, and it was not until the 1954 Sexual Offences Act that there was a practical division between the two. I am not advocating for a step backwards in this regard. The reason for continuing to keep them under separate heads remains the same: whilst offences against the person are aimed at protecting bodily autonomy, sexual offences are concerned with violations of a different kind. Whilst we may be able to consent implicitly to many 'everyday' occurrences as infringements on our bodily autonomy, this is not so

[29] See Chap. 2 for a more detailed analysis of the nature of an experience in the metaverse.

much the case with our sexual autonomy. As a result, there would be no such 'everyday touching' or horseplay exceptions available under the proposed offences as compared to common law assault and battery.[30] The distinction, however, between fear tantamount to the realisation of an outcome and actual realisation of an outcome is the same as present in different unwanted sexual interactions in the metaverse.

Let us return to Nina Jane Patel's experience as an example of sexual assault under the proposed offence:

> I recently shared my experience of sexual harassment in Facebook/Meta's Venues. Within 60 seconds of joining — I was verbally and sexually harassed — 3–4 male avatars, with male voices, essentially, but virtually gang raped my avatar and took photos — as I tried to get away they yelled — "don't pretend you didn't love it" and "go rub yourself off to the photo.
>
> A horrible experience that happened so fast and before I could even think about putting the safety barrier in place. I froze.[31]

Her account is testament to the visceral reactions produced by assault in the metaverse. Certainly, her brain apprehended immediate touching, irrespective of whether such touching could take place. The action was clearly of a sexual nature and seriously impacted her.[32] What is perhaps more concerning is that such an event took place in a game for children. Such experiences may feel more intrusive or unexplainable for younger people, especially in a place advertised as safe and fun.

Let's suppose for a minute that a victim in the same situation as Patel had been wearing a haptic bodysuit. As a result, they would have been able to feel the hands of their assailants on their chest and other parts of their body. This would be classed under the section concerning sexual battery.

The importance of introducing both sections should not be understated. It is recognised and accepted that many academics and members of the public may see sense in an absolute divide between sexual touching and fear of the sexual touching itself, perhaps with criminal liability only arising in the case of the former. However, a combined approach is justified given the changing nature of sexual interaction and the fact that many individuals have been and will likely be subject to the kind of violation described by Patel above. This situation ought still to be covered by the criminal law: but-for the absence of physical touch facilitated through haptic technology, the law would rightly designate it under s.3 SOA 2003, even if the only "physical" outcome was a weak vibration.

It also acts as a double-edged sword, both protecting potential victims and protecting the rights of the defendant. Irrespective of any displayed "haptic status", the sentence that a defendant should receive should not be contingent on whether they happened to attack an individual with or without haptic technology. I would even

[30] For example, consent is a defence in contact sports (*R v Billinghurst* [1978] Crim LR 553), or "rough horseplay" as *in R v Jones (Terence)* (1986) 83 Cr App R 375.

[31] Patel (2021).

[32] I note that 'impact' is not always easy to define or identify. However, given space constraints, to explore this in detail is beyond the scope of the current inquiry.

suggest that, at some point, the two could be assimilated. I have not proposed this here, as it is not easy to predict with certainty how the technology will evolve and how pervasive metaverse sexual interaction may be. However, there may come a time that, in a similar manner to common law assault, both sexual assault and sexual battery could be assimilated under one head of 'sexual assault'.

One criticism that may arise if these are not implemented as a separate chapter in the SOA but rather replace s.1–4 is the potential unwanted effects on sexual offences in the non-virtual world. Considering that sexual battery would replace situations currently classified as sexual assault, most concerns would likely surround the proposed redefinition of sexual assault. There may indeed, at first, appear to be a risk of overcriminalisation. After all, would a sexually suggestive comment and a step towards someone else constitute assault? Possibly, depending on the context.[33] However, I think that such concerns may be overstated. Firstly, the evidential burden would be difficult to overcome outside of the virtual context. To fall under the proposed new offence, the prosecution must prove that the expected touching is sexual. The definition of sexual in s.78 is an objective one.[34] Therefore, even if the victim perceived the potential touching to be sexual, this would not fall under the proposed offence unless it was objectively so. Just reaching in the individuals' vague direction, without more, could not therefore constitute sexual assault. However, any offence not falling under this could still constitute common law assault or harassment. For example, an individual may perceive that looking through a bedroom window was sexual. However, it would instead likely fall under common law assault following *Smith*.[35]

A more powerful criticism is that the definition of sexual assault and sexual battery does not facilitate offences where consent is retroactively vitiated upon discovery of some deception.[36] For example, say that Person A did not wear any haptics and had uncovered the presence of some deception after the sexual activity had taken place. They cannot then say, without the presence of considerable creativity, that they apprehended immediate unwanted touching of a sexual nature. I do not pretend that they could. Instead, I suggest that this could be brought under the alternative offence of "Procurement of Sexual Activity by Deception." This will be discussed further in a later section and the following chapter. For now, it suffices to say that there would be no legal fiction involved, as the intrusion is different. Although there is overlap between the two, the appropriate charge would be the deceptive charge in this case.

---

[33] Words can form the basis of assault under the OAPA, see *R v Ireland* [1997] 3 WLR 534 . A concern could be that if we assimilate OAPA and SOA too closely, this will constitute sexual assault rather than harassment.

[34] Note, it is not without its critics: Ormerod and Laird (2021), p. 817.

[35] *Smith v Chief Constable of Woking Police* [1983] Crim LR 323.

[36] See, for example, R v McNally [2013] EWCA Crim 1051.

4.3.3 *Causing a Person to Engage in Sexual Activity Without Consent*

This would remain largely the same as the current provision, with the same objections as above raised to the penetrative standard currently present in s.4(4). Instead, sexual activity should be taken on its broadest terms to include all the proposed offences without a distinction between penetrative and non-penetrative acts. The primary difference would be to insert a new subsection specifically including hackers within the scope of the offence.

Attacks can be carried out through the avatar of one individual whilst being controlled remotely by another. For example, the situation where Person A and Person B are having a consensual sexual interaction in the metaverse, and Person C hacks into the controls for Person A's avatar without their knowledge, causing non-consensual sexual acts to be performed on Person B, seems exactly the kind that a provision such as s.4 SOA 2003 ought to be able to regulate.

4.3.4 *A Deception Offence*

The Sexual Offences Act 2003 notably omitted to include an updated form of s.3(1) of the Sexual Offences Act 1956, which was as follows:

4.3.4.1 Procurement of a Woman by False Pretences

1. *It is an offence for a person to procure a woman, by false pretences or false representations, to have unlawful sexual intercourse in any part of the world.*[37]

The reasons for this apparent omission are unclear.[38] However, the factual matrixes of the cases themselves have not ceased to be raised before the courts, and the resulting patchwork of case law has at times been called contradictory, discriminatory and dismissive.

Such difficulties within the case law are likely only to be exacerbated by the metaverse. One of the greatest and most promising innovations of the metaverse is its ability to allow us to express ourselves through avatars: we can design and embody the representation of ourselves that we choose. However, as discussed earlier, although the avatars are the representation, it is the controller of the avatar which embodies the representation. Therefore, the issues we are currently facing are effectively translated online whilst social, and indeed sexual, norms change. In this context, we now face new questions.

---

[37] Sexual Offences Act 1956, s.3.

[38] See further Laird (2014), p. 499.

These questions are more comprehensively dealt with in the following chapter on consent. Here, the proposed offence is likely to, and indeed should, bleed into the non-virtual offences as well. It ought to be gender-neutral, but the provisions could broadly replicate the 1956 offence. It would be used to represent the distinct wrong and violation of a retroactive realisation of the offence and the law surrounding conditional consent or cases of sustained deception.

4.3.5 Rape by Penetration

This offence would broadly replicate s.1 and s.2. The current law presents theoretical inconsistencies in its treatment of penetration and sexual offences. Chief among these has been the distinction between rape in s.1 and assault by penetration in s.2.

4.3.5.1 Defining and Requiring Penile Penetration

The law's view of the male sex organ has always been obvious: the penis.[39] However, has not always been equally clear what the law views as the female sex organ. The statute and CPS legal guidance require penetration of the vagina, which is taken to include the vulva.[40] However, as Langston argues, the law's focus has typically been underinclusive:

> *Is the female sex organ the vagina, the clitoris, or the vulva, which includes the vagina and clitoris? If the clitoris is a sex organ, can it be penetrated?*[41]

The importance of answers to such questions is paramount to identify what the law, either explicitly or implicitly, views as so violative to a person's body that it constitutes rape. Perhaps more importantly, it then raises the question of whether such a distinction is justifiable.

In their paper 'Setting the Boundaries' published prior to the enactment of the SOA 2003, the Home Office commented the following on the distinction between penile penetration and other forms of penetration:

> 2.8.4 We were uneasy about extending the definition of rape to include all forms of sexual penetration. We felt rape was clearly understood by the public as an offence that was committed by men on women and on men. We felt that the offence of penile penetration was **of a particularly personal kind**, it carried risks of **pregnancy** and **disease transmission** and should properly be treated separately from other penetrative assaults. We therefore set aside our presumption of gender-neutrality as regards the perpetrator for offences for the crime of rape and propose that it be limited to penile penetration.[42]

---

[39] See s. 1: "intentionally penetrates with his penis..."

[40] S.79(9) SOA 2003.

[41] Langston (1998), p. 14.

[42] Supra (n22), para 2.8.4, emphasis added.

On this reading, there appear to be three main points made, emphasised in bold above, specifically relating to the justification of relying on penile penetration.

The first that the offence was of a "particularly personal kind", merits further consideration. The phrase itself is unexplained and appears to suggest that because it was the invasion of the body by another biological organ, this is worse than penetration by a sex toy or another instrument, such as a bottle. However, if part of the wrong of penetration is the bruising and pain experienced during sex, then this surely occurs irrespective of whether the penetration is penile or something else.[43] There may even be further harm by using another instrument.[44] For example, in some countries, severe and sometimes fatal injuries are frequently sustained by "brutal rape" with other objects, such as beer bottles, gun barrels or sticks.[45] Rape is not just violence. It is terror, it is subjugation, but most of all, it is about power. This remains the case irrespective of whether the penetration is penile or something different.

If, as MacKinnon argues, the law "sees and treats women the way men see and treat women", this distinction between penile penetration and object penetration again appears untenable.[46] If rape and sexual assault are no longer crimes of property but instead rooted in dignity or autonomy, then the justification that penile sex is more personal and thus purports to distinguish two specific harms in s.1 and s.2, despite the same result, ultimately fails. Cynically, this is perhaps a crude attempt at 'fair' labelling: after all, if the affront to dignity is the same, then perhaps one of the only remaining defining differences is the perceived pleasure experienced by the perpetrator. If the offence of penile penetration is "of a particularly personal kind", my question would perhaps be: personal for whom?

As regards the pregnancy and the possibility of STIs, there are a few inconsistencies in the outcome. Firstly, whether protection was used is only considered as a mitigating factor at sentencing rather than an integral harm at the centre of the rape.[47] Furthermore, the transmission of disease does not exclusively occur upon penile penetration. It is perfectly possible to contract an STI orally, through genital touching, through breastfeeding, through sex toys, and blood transfusions.[48] Regarding pregnancy specifically, there is no greater punishment for raping an infertile woman than for a fertile woman. The fertility of the perpetrator equally does not feature in discussions concerning the actus reus of the crime. Such distinctions would rightly be untenable. Justification of the means of identification of a crime by reference to a select few of the harms without wider consideration is

---

[43] Presumably, the remainder of the wrong is the violation of sexual autonomy. This again remains the same.

[44] Penetration by foreign objects could present different harms based on the material. For example, a glass bottle shattering during penetration presents an additional, violative harm that does not present in penile penetration.

[45] The ACQUIRE Project (2006).

[46] MacKinnon (1982), p. 61.

[47] Sentencing Council (2014).

[48] World Health Organisation (n.d.).

equally difficult to conceptually and coherently maintain. Sex is no longer—if it ever was—centred on procreation.

This is further notable considering the sentencing guidelines. The baseline for sentencing is that there is always 'harm' suffered.[49] One of the harms resulting from penetration is listed as "Pregnancy or STI as a consequence of rape" in the sentencing guidelines. Even though it is correct that these are recognised as "principal factual elements", the presence of which at the time of the offence may exacerbate the types of long-term harm suffered by the victim, the sentencing guidelines are far from recognising them as exclusive or even central harms of rape. Instead, they are listed alongside other less tangible elements. In particular, the law recognises the same level of severity when assessing the sentence "physical and psychological harm" and whether the victim had a specific vulnerability.[50] It appears circular to base the justification for biological penetration as the exclusive basis of rape on a select few of the harms used to identify the severity of the offence without further justification beyond the arguments outlined above. Singling out pregnancy and STI transmissions as an explanation for identifying penile penetration as the actus reus of rape appears ill-conceived in this light.

The law's exclusive focus on a phallocentric concept of sex has serious shortcomings. There is little question of intimacy or significance in the context of female same-sex couples who engage in sexual relations without penetration. To be violated by a partner is arguably the pinnacle of betrayal and a severe violation of trust and sexual autonomy. Such a violation is not mitigated by the fact that the partner does not possess a penis.

Interestingly, if it is accepted that the "particularly personal" aspect does in some way relate to penetration by a biological organ, then all three justifications seem to focus little on violations of sexual autonomy. This is interesting when the justification for including oral rape under s.1 is considered:

> 2.8.5 The present crime of rape is limited to the penile penetration of the anus and vagina. Forced oral sex is treated as an indecent assault. We thought that inappropriate. Forced oral sex is **as horrible, as demeaning and as traumatising as other forms of forced penile penetration,** and we saw no reason why rape should not be defined as penile penetration of the anus, vagina or mouth without consent.[51]

This explanation appears markedly different. Instead, the inclusion of forced oral sex seems more centred on the violation of the victim's autonomy and the subsequent harm suffered than exclusively on the potential physical consequences. If this is the underpinning justification, it seems that the explanation given for the inclusion of oral rape is more in line with the spirit of the legislation than the explanation for the elements of the actus reus. This exclusive reliance on physicality in the context of sexual offences has manifested itself detrimentally in other contexts as well.

---

[49] Supra (Sentencing Council 2014)

[50] *Ibid.*

[51] *Ibid.*

In 2023, the Court of Appeal heard argument on the interpretation of the 2012 Criminal Injuries Compensation Scheme ("the Scheme") on appeal from the Upper Tribunal.[52] The argument centred around whether the victim, in this case a 12-year-old boy who had been groomed online, was a victim of a "crime of violence" as defined in paragraph 2(1) of Annex B to the Scheme. Although there was recognition that sexual offences may occur without any touching between the victim and the perpetrator, due to the definition of sexual assault in s.3 of the SOA requiring physical contact, non-touching sexual offences could not fall under the protection of the Scheme. Whilst the court did recognise that the meaning of sexual assault in common language was wider than the statutory definition, the wording of the Scheme and its implicit reference to section 3 of the 2003 act meant that the Scheme had a narrower focus.[53] This was not an entirely satisfactory conclusion as "*it means that a victim of a relatively less serious sexual assault (e.g. leg touching) may be compensated whereas a victim of a more serious sexual offence (e.g. non-touching grooming) is not compensated. This may be counterintuitive as a matter of interpersonal justice, but it appears to be the way in which the scheme currently operates with its focus on "violent" crimes rather than on the consequences upon victims.*"[54]

A consequence of this proposal that may induce criticism is that rape would become a gender-neutral offence. This is not necessarily an unwelcome development and follows the rise in concerns about the treatment of male rape victims under the current system.[55] One other justification advanced by the Home Office was that the public viewed rape as a crime committed by men against women or other men,[56] and that there was insufficient evidence to suggest that penetrative female-on-male sexual violence was the equivalent of rape.[57] In fact, a study conducted in 2023 found that 77% of the British public considered that a woman could rape a man, a statistic rising to 80% when asked if a woman could rape another woman.[58] Some authors have categorised rape as a crime exclusively affecting women, thus entailing the need for a distinction between sexual violence with female and male perpetrators. As McKeever suggests, such a distinction is misleading. It is not incoherent to at once recognise that women experience the wider societal impacts of sexual violence on a collective scale, whereas men do not, whilst also recognising that there are instances where women can be the perpetrators of rape.[59]

---

[52] R(RN) v First Tier Tribunal (Social Entitlement Chamber) and Criminal Injuries Compensation Authority [2023] EWCA Civ 882. In this case, compensation was awarded on a different ground, however, the case demonstrates the narrow applications of the provisions on sexual offences in online contexts.

[53] *Ibid*, at [75]–[76].

[54] *Ibid* at [80].

[55] See further McKeever (2018).

[56] Supra (n22).

[57] Supra (n22), para 2.8.2.

[58] YouGov (2023).

[59] Supra (McKeever 2018), pp. 12–13.

Therefore, although rape is widely—and rightly—recognised as a predominantly gendered crime and the primary group negatively impacted are women, the penetration requirement also negatively impacts anyone who does not conform to patriarchal, heteronormative expectations regarding gender or sexuality. For example, under the current law, a woman who is penetrated by another woman using a sex toy is not legally regarded as a victim of rape but would instead have to seek redress under s.2. Perhaps the issue is less exclusively targeted at women and more focused on maintaining gender roles and expectations which underpin the functioning and efficiency of a patriarchal society.

Assimilating s.1 and s.2 would not only help resolve some inconsistencies in the current law but also allow for situations, as discussed under the current s.1 and 2 involving a meta cam girl, to be labelled rape.

4.3.6 Constructive Rape

This is likely to be the most controversial of the proposed changes. Broadly speaking, the wording would follow the current description of rape found in the Swedish Criminal Code, which allows for rape to be charged where an individual has been forced to endure or undertake:

> another sexual act that, in view of the seriousness of the violation, is comparable to sexual intercourse.[60]

In her explanation of the Swedish offence, Wegerstad clarifies that the starting point for determining what a "sexual act" is, considering the lack of statutory definition, is lasting contact between the perpetrator's body and the victim's genitals or vice versa.[61] However, other acts which do not fulfil these requirements may be covered, provided that "the act had a sexual character and violated the victim's sexual integrity."[62] The determination of a violation comparable to sexual intercourse is admittedly a blurry area. It is broad and deliberately so.[63]

To help balance the harm of the act with the rights of the defence and ensure fair labelling, it would be a constructive offence in the sense that it would require the

---

[60] Swedish Criminal Code, Ch6 It ought to be noted that this has the practical effect in Swedish law of assimilating penile penetration and other forms of penetration. The wording, however, is interesting to consider in the context of the metaverse.

[61] Wegerstad (2021), at ref. 38.

[62] *Ibid.* Swedish law operates through looking at parliamentary minutes and preparatory works to determine the statutory meaning, see Amnesty International (2021).

[63] The breadth of the law has been criticised by rights agencies. For example, after similar legislation was passed in Denmark, the leader of the National Association of Defence Lawyers said that ""You risk convicting someone who objectively shouldn't be convicted because they were unable demonstrate in a sufficiently convincing way that they did nothing wrong in a situation," by moving the burden of proof to the accused. However, these concerns have not been proven, and have been rebutted by academics; see: The Local (2023).

commission of one of the other non-penetrative crimes in the new statute in order to be charged, in a similar vein to constructive manslaughter.

In the 'Setting the Boundaries' paper, the drafters noted that the public perception of rape was broadly aligned with penetration, thus forming part of the justification to make rape a purely penetrative offence.[64] This is partly the reason for the separation here of the penetrative offence and the constructive offence. Although it recognises the practical difficulties that may arise from labelling some sexual interactions in the metaverse 'rape', it also allows for novel forms of sexual interaction to fall within its remit under extreme circumstances. Penetrative acts have become closely associated with rape, may entail a certain social stigma and can be identified as a tool of oppression.[65] Therefore, there is normative merit in maintaining some distinction at this point. We cannot predict with certainty how technology, public perception, and, indeed, the law will develop.

However, the metaverse presents some cases of sexual interaction in which the level of violation and destruction of human sexual autonomy and dignity is so grave and so pervasive that the labels of sexual battery and sexual assault are incapable of encapsulating the crime. I will give you an example.

Cyber brothels are not novel. At their most advanced level, it is possible to rent out a room in Berlin to interact with Kokeshi, a silicon sex doll and interact with it in VR.[66] At their least advanced, they are known as 'condos' in the popular children's game Roblox, where entry is accessible to all users without age verification.[67] In a recent report, Europol asked the question whether:

> … offenders could be virtually brought into a child's room with the ability to actually physically sexually abuse them through the child's haptic devices – without the offenders ever having to leave their homes?[68]

Consider this type of technology in the context of human sex trafficking. There would be no need to move the victims from place to place. They would, for all intents and purposes, become no more than 'real-life' Kokeshi's: forced into wearing haptic equipment and then systematically and continually violated. There is even the potential here for videos to be taken of the struggle, both offline and online and for access to be granted to this "brothel" worldwide. In short, it would be nothing less than the complete and continual destruction of sexual autonomy, agency and dignity. Surely, it should not be that 'sexual battery', which is closer analogous to groping, is expected to do this level of leg work. Fair labelling ought to work both ways, especially if we are serious when we say that a key aim of the law surrounding sexual offences is the protection of sexual autonomy.

This would likely be, to borrow the Swedish terminology, a sexual act that, given the seriousness of violation, is comparable to penetration without consent. It is a

---

[64] Supra (n37), para 2.8.4.

[65] See, for example; MacKinnon (2016), where MacKinnon argues that rape is a crime of equality.

[66] Smith (2024).

[67] Van Homrigh (2022).

[68] Europol (2022), p. 18.

high threshold, but one which ought to be accepted to not close the categories and be open to accommodating novel forms of sexual violation, often capable of developing and spreading far faster than a rigid legal taxonomy can accommodate.

4.4 Conclusion

This chapter has considered the current implications of metaverse technology for the Sexual Offences Act 2003. Considering the minimal amount of interaction that could fall under its remit, it has suggested an alternative framework that may be better suited to the types of sexual interaction facilitated by new technologies.

References

Amnesty International (2021) Criminalization and prosecution of rape in Sweden. https://www.amnesty.org/en/wp-content/uploads/2021/05/EUR4224262020ENGLISH.pdf
Duranske D (2007) Reader Roundtable: "Virtual Rape" Claim Brings Belgian Police to Second Life. https://virtuallyblind.com/2007/04/24/open-roundtable-allegations-of-virtual-rape-bring-belgian-police-to-second-life/
Europol (2022) Policing in the Metaverse: What Law Enforcement Needs to Know. https://www.europol.europa.eu/cms/sites/default/files/documents/Policing%20in%20the%20meta-verse%20-%20what%20law%20enforcement%20needs%20to%20know.pdf
HAL 90210 (2016) Oculus miffed: when VR is so immersive you fall flat on your face. https://www.theguardian.com/technology/2016/nov/30/oculus-vr-immersive-fall-face-plant-virtual-reality
Home Office (2000) Setting the Boundaries: Reforming the Law on Sexual Offences Vol I
Langston L (1998) No penetration—and it's still rape. Pepperdine Law Rev 26(1):1–36
Laird K (2014) Rapist or rogue?: deception, consent and the sexual offences act 2003. Criminal Law Rev 7:492–510
Lynn R (2007) Virtual Rape is Traumatic, but Is It a Crime? https://www.wired.com/2007/05/sexdrive-0504/
MacKinnon C (1982) Feminism, Marxism, method and the state: an agenda for theory. Signs 7(3):515–544
MacKinnon C (2016) Rape Redefined. Harv Law Policy Rev 10(2):431–477
McGlynn C (2024) Towards a new criminal offence of intimate intrusions. Fem Leg Stud 32:189–212
McGlynn C, Rigotti C (2024) Meta-rape: sexual violence, criminal law and the metaverse. Accessible: https://www.claremcglynn.com/_files/ugd/e87dab_c2923fe035b24e47ac77cfd728b44f80.pdf
McKeever N (2018) Can a woman rape a man and why does it matter? Crim Law Philos 13:599–619
Ormerod D, Laird K (2021) Smith, Hogan, and Ormerod's criminal law, 16th edn. Oxford University Press, Oxford
Patel NJ (2021) Reality or Fiction? https://medium.com/kabuni/fiction-vs-non-fiction-98aa0098f3b0
Sentencing Council (2014) Rape. https://www.sentencingcouncil.org.uk/offences/crown-court/item/rape/
Smith N (2024) Concern rises over AI in adult entertainment. https://www.bbc.co.uk/news/articles/c2qqxqgp9yno

The ACQUIRE Project (2006) Traumatic Gynecologic Fistula as a Result of Sexual Violence. https://pdf.usaid.gov/pdf_docs/PNADF980.pdf

The Local (2023) Denmark's sexual consent law 'used as intended' in the first two years. https://www.thelocal.dk/20230317/denmarks-sexual-consent-law-used-as-intended-in-first-two-years#:~:text=The%20law%2C%20which%20requires%20both,considered%20rape%20in%20legal%20trials

Van Homrigh M (2022) Metaverse: Young girls 'virtually raped', new report reveals. https://www.nzherald.co.nz/world/metaverse-young-girls-virtually-raped-new-report-reveals/WNLVTC7CDX5YUAYQSXLP3PDA3Y/

Weare S (2020) The penetrative offence in section 4 of the sexual offences act 2003: offenders, victims, and outcomes after detection. Br J Criminol 60(4):930–948

Weare S, Hulley J (2019) Experiences of men forced-to-penetrate women in the UK: Context, consequences, and engagement with the criminal justice system. https://wp.lancs.ac.uk/forced-to-penetrate-cases/files/2019/07/BA-FTP-project-report-2019.pdf

Wegerstad L (2021) Sex must be voluntary: sexual communication and the new definition of rape in Sweden. German Law J 22(5):734–752

World Health Organisation (n.d.) Sexually Transmitted Infections (STIs). https://www.who.int/health-topics/sexually-transmitted-infections#tab=tab_1

YouGov (2023) What is considered 'rape'? The public's definition differs greatly from the law. https://yougov.co.uk/society/articles/45407-what-considered-rape-publics-definition-differs-gr

Chapter 5
Consent and Deception

5.1 Introduction

An online petition launched in April 2024 sought the implementation of an affirmative consent standard.[1,2] The Government replied: "We have no plans to amend the law on consent. It is long established, well understood by courts, police, practitioners and the public, and provides victims with effective protection from sexual abuse."[3] With respect to the Ministry of Justice, this is simply not true: the public does not have a clear understanding of consent,[4] and the law surrounding it is still a battleground for academics and practitioners alike.[5]

The meaning of consent in sexual offences is contentious, both in academic and public discourse. This is true despite the definition introduced at s. 74 of the Sexual Offences Act 2003.[6] Touted as a form of 'moral magic', in many jurisdictions it is consent which supposedly transforms the violative act of rape into an intimate sexual interaction.[7] However, this orthodox view is not unchallenged, and there is a push internationally to define rape in a way that does not rely on the concept of consent.[8]

---

[1] A consent standard which requires the explicit and fully informed consent of the individual.

[2] Ministry of Justice (2024).

[3] *Ibid.*

[4] YouGov (2018) which found *inter alia* that 33% of Britons think it usually isn't rape when a woman is pressured into having sex without physical violence and 40% consider the removal of a condom without a partner's consent is usually not rape.

[5] Criminal Law Reform Now Network (2021).

[6] S. 74 Sexual Offences Act 2003. For an alternative proposed definition, see the work of the Legal Expert Council (2022), p. 3.

[7] Hurd (1996).

[8] See *Prosecutor v Akayesu*, Case No. ICTR-96-4-T, 2 September 1998, and MacKinnon (2016), esp. pp. 443–450.

R. Procktor, *The Sexual Offences Act 2003 and Virtual Reality*, SpringerBriefs in Law, https://doi.org/10.1007/978-3-032-10397-0_5

Expressions of consent exist on a spectrum. With regard to sexual interaction, we may consent enthusiastically, tiredly, explicitly, implicitly and in a myriad of other ways. Questions abound pertaining to how the law separates consent from submission and where to draw the line between morally regrettable conduct and criminal conduct. Virtual reality (VR) raises these same questions, as well as some distinct considerations.

This chapter will first set out the current law. It will then consider the distinct social context of the metaverse, in particular, the roles played by community guidelines and "netiquette". It will then turn to the definitional difficulties surrounding consent, especially within specific social contexts online. Following this, it will address issues relating to impersonation and conditions placed on consent in an online context. For example, is there a level of deception to be expected in online sexual interactions? If we accept that there can be criminal liability for sexual activity in the metaverse, then how does the case law on deception interact? What about 'gender fraud' cases, where an individual has an avatar representing their gender identity rather than physical representation? It will address the implications of current academic views on deception and the potential for a reintroduction of a procurement offence, as suggested in the previous chapter.

5.2 Current Approaches

5.2.1 Defining Consent: Section 74

The law on consent to sexual relations is found in s.74-76 of the Sexual Offences Act 2003.

Section 74 starts with a definition of consent:

> "...a person consents if he agrees by choice and has the freedom and capacity to make that choice."[9]

This definition appears ill-equipped to deal with complex cases through reliance on concepts which themselves are not defined, such as "freedom" and "capacity".[10] In practice, overcoming a consent-based defence to a criminal charge requires proof that:

- V did not consent to the act
- D did not reasonably believe that V consented.[11]

Of note in this context is the notion of reasonable belief. Before the enactment of the SOA 2003, the House of Lords had held in *Morgan* that the standard of belief

[9] S.74 Sexual Offences Act 2003.

[10] Child et al. (2022), p. 483.

[11] The SOA 2003 changed the statute from an honest belief to a reasonable one.

required was an 'honest' rather than reasonable one.[12] The desire to avoid an argument hinging on a subjectively 'honest' but objectively unreasonable belief helped shape the provision's drafting. However, questions still remain. After all, to whom must the belief be considered reasonable? Equally, what does 'all the circumstances' include? The provision itself, added after Parliament rejected a purely objective test on the grounds that it may be overly harsh on individuals with learning disabilities, has already produced complex case law.[13]

5.2.2 Rebuttable Evidential Presumptions: Section 75

Section 75 provides a series of rebuttable evidential presumptions. It applies if it has been proven that:

(i) D did the relevant act, and
(ii) any of the circumstances listed in s.75(2) were present[14]; and
(iii) D knew these circumstances existed; then:

 (a) V is taken to have not consented and
 (b) D is taken not to have reasonably believed that C consented unless, in either case, sufficient evidence is raised to the contrary.[15]

For example, when violence is used, or V is unable to communicate their consent, s.75 may be invoked.

5.2.3 Conclusive Presumptions: Section 76

Section 76 introduces two conclusive presumptions: if the prosecution can show that D did the act they are accused of and that one of the presumptions applied, V's consent will be vitiated.

These are:

[12] R v Morgan [1976] A.C. 182.

[13] See, for example, *R v Jacobs* [2023] EWCA Crim 1503.

[14] The circumstances covered by s.75 include: actual violence or fear of immediate violence (75(2)(a) and (75(2)(b) respectively), circumstances where V was unlawfully detained whereas D was not (75(2)(c)), if V was asleep or unconscious at the time of the relevant act (75(2)(d)), where C's physical disability prevents them from being able to communicate to D their consent at the time of the relevant act (75(2)(e)), and finally where V has caused or administered a substance without V's consent which was capable of causing or enabling C to be stupefied or overpowered at the time of the relevant act(75(2)(f)).

[15] Crown Prosecution Service (2021).

(i) That D intentionally deceived V as to the nature or purpose of the relevant act ('the **deception** presumption')
(ii) That D intentionally induced V to consent to the relevant act by impersonating a person known personally to V ('the **impersonation** presumption')

A deception falling outside the scope of s.76 may still vitiate consent, as it may also contravene the general definition of consent under s.74.[16]

The remainder of this chapter will address some of the issues likely to arise in the context of the metaverse, focusing primarily on issues falling under s.76 and s.74.[17]

5.3 Framing Consent in the Metaverse

5.3.1 Community Guidelines and Netiquette

Community guidelines predominantly exist to prevent unwelcome behaviour between individuals. Although all users must accept to abide by them upon joining a platform, they are generally not legally enforceable. A player in breach may be banned from the game for a period or indefinitely, but they will not be taken to court for breaching the community guidelines unless their behaviour falls within the scope of the laws of their jurisdiction.[18] Content which violates these guidelines may be taken down. Although there is some evidence to suggest that there is a consensus on which content needs to be taken down, many critics reject this idea of 'moderation' as a form of 'censorship'.[19]

The Information Commissioner's Office requires that social media companies uphold their standards, setting community rules and conditions of use for users of the service and actively upholding or enforcing those rules and conditions.[20] This involves upholding both behaviour policies and content policies.[21]

However, large tech companies are coming under increased scrutiny concerning their enforcement, or more specifically, *lack of* enforcement, regarding community guidelines and the protection of children. For example, the National Crime Agency recently issued an urgent warning following a considerable increase in financially motivated sexual extortion ("sextortion").[22] Experts, such as Paul Raffile, are currently campaigning for greater transparency from tech companies and their

---

[16] *R(F) v DPP* [2014] QB 581.

[17] This is not to suggest that s.75 may not play a role, but it is unlikely to be as substantially impacted by the metaverse and therefore will not be discussed at length in this chapter.

[18] For an interesting look at the prospect of "cyber banishment" as punishment, see Mamak (2023).

[19] Aguerri et al. (2023), and see more broadly: *Moody v Net Choice*, LLC, No. 22277 (U.S. July 1 2024).

[20] Information Commissioners Office (n.d.).

[21] *Ibid.*

[22] National Crime Agency (2024).

For example, VexRuby's website states simply that "Consent is Sexy!" without any further explanation of the concept. Consent may well be 'sexy', but there is no indication of precisely what the company takes that to mean.

Even if there was such a definition, how forceful would it be in cases of violation where the definition offered by the company is overinclusive or underinclusive? For example, if Person A had been accused of a meta-sexual offence against Person B, who resisted but was too frightened to speak, could they rely on a provision in the community guidelines stating that "Consent in this metaverse means that the other party does not say no" to argue that there was consent? Inversely, companies could set the boundary far higher: "Consent means that the other individual verbally confirms their consent to each specific sexual act decided on by the involved parties." Here, skipping a single step, verbal confirmation and discussion of *every* specific sexual act to be performed could render an interaction definitionally non-consensual, whilst the current law would treat it as consensual. It is both undesirable and unlikely that such a course of action would be taken.

However, this again shows the pressing need to consider such interactions as "real" and capable of being dealt with under criminal law, not contract law.[29] Presumably, agreeing to the community guidelines does not override the statutory definition of consent. It seems undesirable to offer tech companies quasi-state status or be capable of drafting community guidelines to suggest that "anything goes." Such an approach may encourage development in the opposite direction, with companies competing to offer the least regulated metaverse or with lower standards of consent to encourage people to join their servers.[30] This is already visible on some online platforms in the context of freedom of speech, such as Truth Social, Telegram and X.[31]

Although community guidelines may not be legally enforceable, they are persuasive in guiding conduct and shaping the type of social interaction occurring between users. Further research is required to help determine how far companies can moderate interactions and where the law ought to step in.

The key takeaway is that virtual worlds are influenced by social norms in the non-virtual but exist within a different context, which is dictated by both the purpose of the virtual space and the norms established by the people accessing it. As a result, a metaverse created exclusively for sexual purposes has significantly different rules and expectations than one created for children's education.[32]

---

[29] The contract being rooted in the user agreement or contract between company and user.

[30] My thanks to Lauren Fox for pointing this out.

[31] For example, on TruthSocial: "Truth+" advertisement stating that "**Free speech lives on Truth+**, where you can watch the news you trust and shows and movies that Big Media has tried to blacklist." (emphasis added). https://help.truthsocial.com/truth-plus/introduction-to-truth-plus/.

[32] As will be discussed later, this may affect the way that we examine what consent in "all the circumstances" looks like.

5.4 Age, Roleplay and Consent

Children and young people express the most interest in metaverse technologies.[33] Most of those are more technologically literate than their parents or guardians.[34] The avatars that they operate, however, are objectively ageless,[35] but may be designed to be perceived as a certain age. Therefore, an individual aged thirty could enter one metaverse as a white-haired, elderly woman and 10 min later join an interactive game as a seven-year-old boy. It is equally possible that they may not seek to be perceived as any age at all but instead present themselves in an imagined way, for example, in the form of animals, both real and imagined. Most, but not all, avatars are created by their users and capable of being modified. They are not constant but ever-changing.

Recent cases already illustrate the types of argument that may be made by the defence where a child embodies an adult avatar and subsequently engages in, or is forced into, some form of sexual interaction in the metaverse. Take, for example, *R v Halsall*.[36] The applicant appealed his conviction by a jury of offences under s.15A (attempted sexual communication with a child) and s.14 (attempting to arrange or facilitate the commission of a child sex offence) SOA 2003. The facts were as follows.[37] The applicant was a 76-year-old man who had created a profile on the online dating app Grindr, a platform predominantly targeted at gay men. On this app, he matched with a profile named "Fun Fun Fun". Kai, the user behind "Fun Fun Fun", told the applicant that he was 14. His picture showed a bare-chested young man on a bed. The profile was, in fact, part of a series of profiles created by an undercover police officer.

The conversation between them soon became graphically sexual, culminating in plans to meet, where the applicant was arrested by the police in possession of a condom and lubricant. During his interview, the applicant made several arguments as to why he believed that Kai was 18 and not 14, as he had stated.

Firstly, the applicant relied on the fact that Grindr was an app for 18-year-olds and upwards, and the creation of an account required a credit card. Secondly, he argued that Kai's style of communication was far more mature than what he would have expected of a 14-year-old. Additionally, he suggested that the profile photo "looked over 18."[38]

Consider if this interaction had occurred in the metaverse, where Kai was not an undercover police officer but instead a 14-year-old boy. Could Halsall feasibly rely on the fact that a condition for entry to the specific metaverse was being over 18?

---

[33] YouGov (2022), pp. 7–9.

[34] Eurostat (2024).

[35] Or at least ageless in any regular sense of the term. We may be able to measure the "age" of an avatar from the date of its creation.

[36] [2024] EWCA Crim 1007.

[37] *Ibid,* found at [6]-[20] of the judgement.

[38] *Ibid,* [13] and [18].

For example, were the metaverse to be one specifically designed for making connections to explore certain kinks consensually, could a defendant argue that they thought the victim's confession as to their age was part of a consensual exploration of kink? It would seem undesirable to suggest that this would be the case, but judging by cases already before the courts, it may well be a claim that is frequently raised.

In the metaverse context, it may be that defendants rely on the fact that specific environments are marketed to, and only supposed to be accessible by, individuals over the age of 18. This may come into an assessment of consent in "all the circumstances", but judging by the current approach of the courts, it is unlikely to be determinative. Such an approach is merited in situations such as *Halsall* above. It may be more difficult in a case whereby D specifically asks V their non-virtual age, and they reply with a fake age above 18.

Cases like these also raise the question of a 'roleplaying defence.' This was implicit in *Halsall* but overt in *BNE*.[39] *BNE* concerned an appeal against conviction for attempted sexual communication with a child and attempting to incite a child to engage in sexual activity following the operation of an undercover police officer. Of particular interest is the precise nature of the appellant's argument that:

> he had at all times believed he was communicating with an adult who was pretending to be only 14 as part of a role-playing fantasy. He gave evidence to that effect. He relied on the facts that [the platform] was aimed at adults and X's profile stated that she was 18. He also relied on features of X's messages such as her use of language, punctuation and grammar, and her professed liking for certain musicians. He further relied on X's profile picture, and the images provided by X, all of which, he asserted, showed what he believed to be a woman aged around 19-23. He pointed to the fact that in each of those images X's face was partially obscured, which he regarded as consistent with his belief that she was an adult engaged in role-playing.[40]

The precise point on appeal was that the jury had not been told the true age of the individual in the photo on the profile to preserve the anonymity of the undercover officer. Whilst the trial judge held that there was a *prima facie* right to disclosure of the true age of the individual in the photo, on the facts, it was determined that it was not in the public interest.[41] This was overturned by the Court of Appeal. In their judgment, whether the image of the person was of an underage individual was important for the jury to appreciate in their deliberations.[42] They did so with particular reference to the applicant's main defence, that he reasonably believed that this was an act of "roleplay".[43,44]

---

[39] [2023] EWCA Crim 1242, the facts are set out at paras [1]-[12].

[40] *Ibid.* at [5].

[41] Supra (n39) at [10].

[42] Supra (n39), see the reasoning at paras [22]-[30]. This case also raises some very interesting questions concerning digital modification of images and their implications, but which do not fall within the scope of the present work.

[43] Supra (n39), to this point see [30].

[44] Note that this does not imply that that defence will be successful, but that the age of the individual in the photo may assist the jury in coming to their conclusions.

This is notable for two reasons. Firstly, it raises the same questions as above relating to the age of access to certain online spaces, in metaverses which may be developed for consensual explorations of kink.[45] This is a weak defence: paedophilia is not a kink.[46] It does, however, raise broader questions relating to what conduct should—or perhaps more importantly, should not—be allowed in the metaverse outside of the context of minors. For example, should fantasies relating to bestiality, where one user has an animal avatar, also be banned? Secondly, it places under the spotlight a wider question relating to the hyper-sexualisation of young women and girls and the way that the pornography industry has exploited this as 'desirable' or 'able to be corrupted'. Adult actresses are often portrayed wearing schoolgirl uniforms, with their hair in bunches and minimal makeup to replicate young girls. If they are over the age of 18, this is perfectly legal.[47] However, it does raise questions as to how distinguishable it may be in cases with facts less clear-cut than *Halsall*. For example, would objectively child-like behaviour or language be enough to call into question whether D reasonably believed that V was under the age of 18? Or could it be said to be some form of 'roleplay' or flirtation? The 'roleplaying' defence is clearly, and rightly, a weak one. But it is propped up by a dominant narrative spun by the pornography industry that hypersexualises youth, inexperience and innocence as 'desirable'.

5.5 Deception

Much ink has been spilt on the complex relationship between deception, mistake and consent in English and Welsh law.[48] The purpose of this chapter is not to contribute a new perspective to this debate. It is to instead test different viewpoints and see what sexual interaction in the metaverse reveals about them and to uncover some vital areas of research in light of future innovations in the metaverse.

Perhaps one of the only areas of general agreement in the literature is that deception should be capable of vitiating consent under some circumstances. That is generally where the agreement ends, and debates ensue over which behaviour ought to be criminalised and precisely how to label such offences.

This section will first address some of the primary issues in analysing deceptive sexual conduct in the metaverse: the prevalence of deceptive conduct online and

[45] 'Kink' here is being used in a very wide sense.

[46] It ought to be said that similar questions can be raised outside the context of age, where kinks relating to consensual-non-consent (CNC) fantasies are often discussed. There is, I think, a legal distinction here, as in CNC neither one of the parties' capacity is in question. This is distinct from any moral arguments to be made on this subject. For an interesting look at classifying paedophilia, see Dreger (2010).

[47] Although, one may want to question the potential wider impacts of this practice.

[48] Most recently, see CRLNN report in which 13 leading academics give diverging opinions on how the law related to deception ought to be reformed, supra (Criminal Law Reform Now Network 2021).

difficulties with identifying the object of the deception. It will then turn to potential applications of the current provisions under the SOA in the context of the metaverse, particularly as relates to impersonation, deceptions as to purpose, and conditional consent.

5.5.1 *Deceptive Conduct Online*

Phenomena already discussed, such as the Proteus Effect, contribute to the experience of users online, allowing them to "create a separate identity with minimal legal or ethical consequences."[49,50] Gen Z seem to be making the most of this; in a recent survey, 46% of 2000 members of Gen Z interviewed reported "leading a double life" online.[51]

Further studies conclude that there is clear evidence of a direct relationship between anonymity and digital aggression[52]; this follows a line of research since 1969 that shows a link between anonymity and abusive behaviour offline.[53] Anonymity is both a benefit and drawback of sexual interaction online. Whilst allowing a high level of individualism and freedom, it also presents its dangers.

Acceptance of relationships formed and conducted exclusively online is also growing: one study in 2018 found that 20% of children aged 11-16 would be happy having an "online-only" relationship, and 10% of those who had had a boyfriend or girlfriend online said that they had only ever communicated virtually.[54] Often, individuals in online relationships feel the same deep affection and attachment as anyone else. However, virtual relationships, even those that remain exclusively online, may still have disastrous consequences.

In 2020, the results of an inquest into the death of Renae Marsdon were published by the State Coroners' Court of New South Wales.[55] The manner of death is listed as "[deliberately slipping] from the clifftop with the intent to end her life after the termination of a relationship with a person whose identity and intent were, unbeknownst to her, a fabrication created and perpetrated to exercise coercion and control over her by a known person, who engaged in conduct known as "Catfishing."[56] It was later discovered that her partner of 2 years did not exist and was a fictitious persona created by her closest friend, who "was unable to tolerate Renae having an

---

[49] Dwivedi et al. (2023), p. 2072.

[50] For a discussion on the proteus effect, see Chaps. 2 and 3. The seminal paper in this field is Yee and Bailenson (2007).

[51] Raiken (2024).

[52] Kim et al. (2023).

[53] Zimbardo (1969); For an overview, see Dawson (2018)

[54] Internet Matters (2018).

[55] Coroners Court of New South Wales (2020).

[56] *Ibid*, p. 2.

intimate relationship."[57] The coroner found that "Renae was sexually intimate with Brayden, including phone sex, sending him videos and photographs."[58] It is unknown whether Renae was aware of the deception at the time of her death. Evidence indicates that she was not. It is, in any case, a stark reminder of the very real feelings involved in relationships formed online—even where there has been no non-virtual contact.

Recent research has also emphasised the positive role played by identity concealment in some spaces: "Some people navigate the world with the freedom to fully express themselves as they feel they authentically are. Others do not have that luxury."[59] Online spaces can be healing for marginalised and stigmatised groups, for example, the LGBTQ+ community:

> Avatar creation can be a literal lifesaver. It enables people who may live in areas where it's too dangerous to do so, or people who just aren't in a good enough financial situation, to still be allowed to be who they truly are... I can't count the amount of times I've felt gender euphoria simply from being in my avatar and seeing myself move around in it.[60]

In the growing number of cases addressing technology-facilitated sexual offences, some reliance has been placed on the prevalence of deception online. In *Halsall*,[61] it is of interest to note that the applicant asserted that he justifiably believed the person he was communicating with was above the age of 18, despite conversations stating that the person was 14, as "he thought around 50% of people on Grindr[62] lied about their age."[63] This was, quite rightly, rejected.[64] However, it is an interesting first glance at how the courts may tackle claims or beliefs concerning the prevalence of deception online.

5.5.2 *The Subject of the Deception: Deceptive Users or Deceptive Avatars?*

The second issue meriting discussion before consideration of specific provisions is whether the deception must relate to the individual controlling the avatar or to the avatar itself. As discussed previously, the actor ought to be separated from the avatar.[65]

---

[57] Supra (Coroners Court of New South Wales 2020) at [63].

[58] Supra (Coroners Court of New South Wales 2020) at [65].

[59] Le Forestier and Lewis (2024).

[60] Gladwin (2024).

[61] Supra (n36); the same could be said for disabled people who use virtual spaces as their primary space for social interaction, see Boellstorff (2020).

[62] A free dating app for the LGBTQ+ community predominantly used by gay men.

[63] Supra (n36) at [19].

[64] *Ibid.*, reasons given at [44].

[65] See the discussion in Chap. 2.

The separation must necessarily be maintained in cases of deception. This is not to deny the importance of the avatar to some users.[66] Indeed, recognition of the avatar as oneself may be instrumental in promoting and maintaining the user's sense of embodiment.[67] However, avatars are necessarily customisable and rely on a variable amount of input from the individual user. For example, a person may buy or use a premade avatar designed by the platform and generally available to all users upon entry to the online space. They may instead play a large role in designing their avatar, customising it to look exactly like themselves or exactly how they wish to be perceived. Alternatively, they may create the most absurd purple-skinned, orange-haired, green-horned avatar to represent themselves in the digital world.

Therefore, it is important to bear in mind the distinction between avatar and user. The avatar is not autonomous. Avatars are primarily a form of property, used as a tool which both represents and helps embody the individual presence in the virtual world.[68] That does not dismiss the cases where avatars do have a special significance to their users but rather helps to define the scope of the current inquiry: only deceptions that pertain to the user, and not the avatar, ought to interest the criminal law.

This does not preclude an individual from using their avatar to induce a belief about their non-virtual self. However, it seems unreasonable to expect all individuals to create entirely accurate avatars. Indeed, creativity in self-expression is one of the benefits of the metaverse.

5.5.3 Impersonation

Section 76 requires that V know the victim 'personally'.[69] It is well established that impersonation of a significant other vitiates consent.[70] However, if the impersonation is either (a) of someone unknown to V or (b) is not instrumental in inducing the sexual activity itself, the impersonation presumption in section 76 cannot be relied upon.[71] It is equally open to the jury to find that impersonation vitiates consent under s.74, especially given that s.76 is rarely applied.[72]

This raises two interlocking issues if we are going to assess impersonation as capable of precluding consent in the metaverse. Firstly, it raises a question as to whether it is possible to know someone 'personally' when interactions have exclusively taken place online. Secondly, it requires considering the distinction between

[66] For example, a trans-person being able to experience living as their preferred gender facilitated through the medium of the avatar.

[67] See the discussion in Chap. 2.

[68] Fauchoux and Bruguière (2024).

[69] S.76 Sexual Offences Act 2003.

[70] *R v Elbekkay* [1995] Crim LR 163.

[71] S.76 SOA 2003, although they may be able to achieve a similar result through recourse to s.74.

[72] *R v Bingham* [2013] EWCA Crim 823, at [24].

'genuine' online profiles (profiles created by Person A, presenting as Person A) and 'fictional' online profiles (profiles created by Person A, purporting to be Person B or an entirely fictional person).

What does it mean to know someone "personally"? Simester and Sullivan suggest that it requires Person A to be able to distinguish Person B from anyone else in the world.[73] In this way, the requirement centres on the presence of a relationship between the two individuals rather than any objective 'personal knowledge' of another. Certainly, the personal relationship between two individuals who exclusively communicate daily online is no less valuable than two friends who see each other and communicate every day. In both cases, there is a clear personal relationship between the two. This also explains the reason why impersonation of a celebrity not personally known to V does not fall under this section: knowledge based on purely physical characteristics does not equate to personal knowledge for the purposes of s.76. Clearly, knowing someone personally is about more than being able to pick them out of a crowd but connected to the relationship between the individuals. Acknowledging how our relationships shape our personhood allows for a far richer understanding of "impersonation", which may prove invaluable as our social lives increasingly take place in virtual spaces.[74]

Therefore, as Simester and Sullivan argue, given the prevalence of online dating in modern society, there is "no good reason to restrict impersonation to physical acquaintances":

> Suppose that A (a real person) creates a genuine online profile and interacts with V. D logs on to A's online account and arranges to meet with V. V thinks D to be A and willingly has sex with D under that misapprehension.[75]

This, as they suggest, is not a "stretch of language."[76] By assuming the place of A in A and V's relationship, D has clearly deceived V. However, it leaves open a distinction between the purely online interaction between the D and V in the metaverse in comparison to Simester and Sullivan's hypothetical. In a virtual space where identities can exist entirely online, is the fact that this 'online identity' has no legal existence in the form of an identity card or birth certificate decisive? The individual operating the avatar will retain their non-virtual identity. However, this does not mean that their online identity could not be assumed as a separate matter. For example, it is entirely conceivable that D could assume the identity of Username2394 online, operating their avatar, without ever assuming the identity of Mr. Smith from London.

---

[73] Supra (Child et al. 2022), pp. 484–486.

[74] See on the need for a relational understanding of personhood concerning impersonation in s.76 SOA, Farah (2023), in particular at pp. 67–84.

[75] *Ibid.*

[76] *Ibid.*

In *Devonald*,[77] the prosecution could not rely on the s.76 impersonation presumption[78]: 'Cassey', the girl V believed himself to be communicating with, did not exist.[79]A similar situation occurred in *Bingham*. Here, D created two fictitious personas to extort his girlfriend into sending explicit photos and then to blackmail her. Again, s.76 would be unlikely to have worked: the individuals were created by the extorter as fictitious personalities for his criminal purpose. In cases such as the above, the courts have generally relied on deceptions as to the nature or purpose of the act rather than impersonation. Could interactions in the metaverse challenge this distinction?

Consider the following:

Scenario One
Person A has been in a six-month online relationship with Person B. B's brother, C, decides one day to use his headset and log into his online account. A, seeing that "B" is online, logs on and starts flirting with him. C knows of A and her relationship with B. A notices something different about "B" and asks him if everything is okay as he is behaving differently. C, as "B", replies that there is nothing wrong and he is just feeling a bit under the weather. They engage in sexual activity. The next day, B logs onto the platform, and A refers to what she understands as their previous interaction. B is shocked and informs her that it was his brother, C.

This ought to be a case of impersonation: B is known personally to A, and C has used that relationship to deceive A into sexual activity. B's online identity is not merely fictional. Admittedly, the lines here may not be easy to draw. However, consider by way of contrast the following:

Scenario Two
Person A had a one-time sexual interaction with 'User1383483' a week ago. It was so incredible that they have been looking for this user since. Person A waits at the same place where they met them the first time, see their avatar and their username, and subsequently engage in sexual activity. Following this, A comments on their previous experience as this one was not as enjoyable. User1383483 responds that it may have been his brother, as they share an account.

It would likely be said that Person A did not know User1383483 "personally", and therefore, it would not be a case of impersonation: Person A had nothing to distinguish this user from anyone else in the world.[80] Perhaps there could be an argument that the individual username is enough to distinguish the user? I doubt it. Usernames are usually assigned to the account, not the individual user. After all,

[77] [2008] EWCA Crim 527.

[78] Although, note that they were able to rely on a deception as to the nature or purpose of the act under s.74 instead.

[79] Supra (Child et al. 2022), p. 485.

[80] Supra (Child et al. 2022), p. 486.

avatars are modifiable and users interchangeable: changing either does not require an individual to change the name on their account.

However, how to distinguish *Devonald* and *Bingham*, where there is clearly no impersonation, from cases such as Scenario One? I argue that there is a distinction—and it is a justifiable one. In both *Devonald* and *Bingham*, the fictitious personalities had been created and used for the sole purpose of perpetrating a criminal act. However, in Scenario One, B's use of the avatar had been to forge an online identity and create social or amorous connections. A relationship had been formed between A and B to the extent that they knew each other 'personally'. This identity had then been assumed by another and intentionally used to deceive. Perhaps another technology-based example is the distinction between a scammer creating an email address to deceive people into sending money and a hacker sending an email from a bank executive's email address to their customers asking them to deposit their money into a different account. One is created entirely fictitiously; one is the use of an online representation of a specific individual's identity.

There are, admittedly, difficulties with this approach. For example, what is the solution if a person shares a headset or account with friends or family? It is difficult to hold that there could be some form of impersonation of a collective identity. It seems unlikely that an individual could know a user personally when an avatar is shared. Whether they could be deceived into thinking that they have a personal connection with one individual when there are multiple is another question entirely and would likely not rest upon the impersonation presumption.

The second difficulty is where the 'impersonator' is unaware of the mistaken identity. Such cases are exceptionally rare in the non-virtual world but could arise in cases such as the one in Scenario Two in the virtual world. Under s.74 SOA, D would likely have the defence that they reasonably believed that V consented, as they were unaware of the mistaken identity. It may be different if A makes a comment prior to sexual activity about their previous encounter, and B affirms her identification of them, but in practice, this is unlikely to occur.

This is an area which requires further investigation, especially as the number of relationships formed purely online and acceptance of such relationships is growing.

5.5.4 Purpose

Current case law suggests that a deception as to the purpose of the act may only be invoked under s.76 when V is *entirely* deceived as to D's purpose. Thus, causing sexual activity for the *pure* purpose of humiliation may fall under deception as to purpose,[81] causing sexual activity for both humiliation and sexual gratification is not.[82]

[81] Supra (n77).

[82] Supra (n72).

Here is one example of how deception as to purpose may operate in the metaverse.

Scenario Three
A and B are playing a large multiplayer role-playing game in the metaverse together. A is not very experienced at the game, and so is relying on B as someone with more experience. B tells A that to progress to the next level, they must engage in sexual activity.[83] A subsequently engages in sexual activity with B, only finding out later that he lied to her and there was no reason for the sexual interaction.

How ought the law to deal with this situation? Did A realise that this was for the purpose of sexual gratification?

There is an interesting parallel to be drawn here with *R v Matt*.[84] In this case, D had purported to be a director for an acting company and deceived V into sexual activity as part of a casting for the television show Basic Instinct. D was, in fact, a plumber. Here, the court distinguished *Bingham*, arguing instead that V was still deceived as she had agreed to simulated sexual arousal and had not in any part appreciated that D was engaging in genuine sexual arousal. As a result, her consent was vitiated. A similar approach could be taken in the scenario above concerning simulated sexual arousal to unlock a new level of a game and genuine sexual arousal. However, in light of the narrow constructions often given to s.76 presumptions, this is unlikely to stretch far. Instead, the approach in *Bingham*, that there need only be some recognition or understanding of the purpose of sexual arousal, is likely to apply in the majority of cases. Indeed, the precise type of metaverse may play a role in this. The broad stroked brush used by the court to identify deception as to the purpose of the act may, therefore, lend itself to an equally broad argument: could it be argued that in a metaverse designed for sexual interaction, there will virtually always be awareness that any sexual interaction will likely have some purpose of sexual gratification?[85] This makes s.76 difficult to invoke in many contexts. Therefore, s.74 may be preferred.

5.5.5 *Mistakes, Deception and Consent*

Deceptions as to the nature of the act have been given a narrow focus in the current law.[86] Many of the issues arise in relation to placing conditions on characteristics of a sexual partner: "where the victim has placed, or would have placed, a condition on

[83] This is sometimes, and increasingly, the case in many games. See, for example: Gods of War 3, RapeLay, and RapeDay for games where sexual offences must be carried out in order to advance to the next level, or as an integral feature of the game.

[84] [2015] EWCA Crim 162.

[85] Note that this is only in reference to vitiating consent on the idea that V did not appreciate the purpose. Merely accessing a metaverse intended for sexual interaction should never be considered implicit consent to any form of sexual activity.

[86] *R v Lawrence* [2020] EWCA Crim 1971.

the characteristics of the other person with whom they are engaging in sexual intercourse."[87] The case law under this limb is incoherent: whilst non-disclosure of HIV status,[88] deliberate concealment of a profession,[89] or an active deception as to fertility[90] does not vitiate consent, non-disclosure of sex at birth will.[91] This is primarily the limb under which issues will arise in the metaverse.

The tensions in the current law are most clearly highlighted in the heavily criticised decision in *Lawrence*.[92] The facts were as follows.[93] D met V on a dating website, where they exchanged sexually explicit messages and phone calls. During one of these exchanges, D represented to V that he had had a vasectomy. This representation was repeated when they subsequently met at V's house. Following intercourse, D sent a message: "I have a confession. I'm still fertile. I'm sorry."

The prosecution's argument was initially successful: deliberate deception vitiated the complainant's consent. Reversing this, the Court of Appeal instead followed D's argument: as a matter of law, deception as to fertility did not vitiate consent even if relied upon by the claimant as it was not sufficiently closely connected to the nature of the sexual act.[94] Following a review of the arguments and authorities, Lord Burnett concluded that although the jury had found that the complainant had materially relied upon the defendant's deception, "the 'but for' test is insufficient of itself to vitiate consent. There may be many circumstances in which a complainant is deceived about a matter which is central to her choice to have sexual intercourse."[95]

In rejecting a 'but-for' approach, the Court reiterated its previous stance that conditions capable of precluding an individual's consent could be determined through a 'common sense' analysis rather than by reference to the specific preferences of each individual: some deceptions, such as wealth, age or marital status, would "obviously not be sufficient to vitiate consent."[96] The Court of Appeal thus aligned itself with prior case law concerning the disclosure of HIV status,[97] at the same time as distinguishing other cases involving a deception as to the nature of the

---

[87] Alencar (2021), p. 3.

[88] *R v B* [2007] 1 WLR 1567.

[89] *R(Monica) v DPP* [2018] EWHC 3508(QB), where an environmental activist argued that her consent had been vitiated as D had not revealed that he was an undercover policeman.

[90] Supra (n85).

[91] *R v McNally* [2013] EWCA Crim 1051.

[92] Supra (n86).

[93] Supra (n86) at [3]-[7].

[94] Supra (n86) at [34].

[95] Supra (n86) at [34].

[96] Supra (n91) at [24].

[97] Supra (n88).

act, such as taking off the condom during intercourse,[98] or refusing to withdraw during ejaculation.[99]

This section will be divided into two parts. The first will address which 'key facts' ought to merit the attention of the law and how this may operate in the metaverse. The second will consider the current case law's emphasis on the physicality of the deception, especially as it relates to deceptions as to gender, and how sexual interaction in the metaverse may challenge the underlying reasoning of such cases.

5.5.6 No Such Thing as "Trivial" Deception

Academics have suggested different ways to deal with the current incoherence. On one view, it has been argued that if V was mistaken as to a 'key fact' which had V known about, they would not have consented, then there is no consent.[100] Such proposals take the view that it is not for the courts to determine what is 'trivial' in the eyes of the law, all that ought to matter is whether V's sexual autonomy has been violated—a fact that remains true irrespective of the perceived absurdity to external observers. Although this is an "apparently attractive bright line",[101] it has received great criticism for the possibility that it may drastically enlarge the current scope of criminal liability for sexual offences.[102]

Concerns surrounding overcriminalisation have led other scholars to reconsider sexual autonomy as the basis for sexual offences entirely.[103] Towards the middle ground, approaches have been rooted in different concepts of sexual autonomy balanced against other rights. Kennedy, for example, argues that we ought to root our understanding of sexual autonomy in the self-perception of an individual's identity,[104] whereas Palmer instead discusses the law's role in ensuring "freedom to negotiate" in sexual encounters.[105]

Adopting a rigid categorical approach in the metaverse may cause some difficulty. Firstly, because the physical aspect of the sexual act itself may look profoundly different.[106] Secondly, because social norms will be altered, a 'common sense' approach to which deceptions vitiate consent and what is sufficient may prove more difficult.[107] Equally, a rigid categorical approach to sexual offences has

---

98 *Assange v Swedish Prosecution Authority* [2012] UKSC 22.

99 Supra (n88) and supra (n86) at [41].

100 Herring (2005), reiterated in Herring (2021) albeit rooted in different arguments.

101 Dyson (2021), p. 41.

102 Bohlander (2007) and Gross (2007).

103 Rubenfeld (2013), and see in response: Chiesa (2017) and Dougherty (2013a).

104 Kennedy (2021a), and see more recently Kennedy (2024).

105 Palmer (2021).

106 See Chaps. 2 and 4 on this.

107 Especially when the 'common sense' is dictated by non-virtual social norms.

already failed to keep up with developments in technology and the way that they change sexual norms in society.[108]

One response to the Court's approach is to emphasise the absolute nature of V's sexual autonomy. The argument here is that V is best placed to determine their sexual preferences. Therefore, where they identify "dealbreakers" or "bright lines" that they wish to draw, the law ought not to prevent them from doing so.[109] If, as Herring argues, it is never the law's place to decide what a 'trivial' matter is to an individual, how are deceptions identified and held to be capable of precluding consent in the metaverse where deception is so prevalent?

For example, some studies suggest that up to 57% of people on dating websites lie about aspects of their person online, primarily about their names, marital status, location and appearance.[110] Knowing someone online is similar to knowing them offline, but it is by no means identical. Often, online profiles are "idealised" versions of an individual, the individual as they wish to be seen rather than as they are. Equally, as explored above, they can be an outlet or form of self-expression—especially for vulnerable or isolated groups.[111] On an expansive view, all social media or online dating profiles could be a form of deception.

The response would be that this kind of issue is at the heart of the problem: deception is seen as normalised in relationships and, in the cases of idealised hyper-masculine James Bond-style heroes, brushed off as seduction when it is, in fact, a serious harm.[112] Some opponents of this view do not disagree that deception is normalised, just that it is necessarily harmful. For example, Bohlander argues that criminalising every white lie told as part of a seduction paints a naïve picture of women who, according to him, accept that there are risks in sexual interactions.[113] Others, such as Gross, argue that we ought to separate the moral reprehensibility of such deceptions from legal wrongs.[114] However, this common sense approach not only leads to incoherence, as demonstrated by *Lawrence* but may perhaps ironically be the one which imposes a common morality. By delineating what may or may not be integral to an individual's choice to consent to sexual interaction, the court inevitably substitutes its perspective for that of the initial decision maker.

Were Herring's expansive approach to be adopted in the metaverse, there would need to be an increased emphasis on the reasonableness of D's belief in consent. Admittedly, this may just be moving at what stage the 'common sense' test is applied. However, the safeguard would be in place to protect D where, even in the presence of a 'dealbreaker' fact (however trivial it may be), D did not know or could not reasonably have known that the fact was a 'dealbreaker'. Thus, if Person A has

---

108 See Chap. 3 on the need for an "intimate intrusions" offence.

109 Supra (n101) and Dougherty (2013b).

110 Golovina (2017).

111 See supra (Gladwin 2024).

112 Herring (2009), p. 1.

113 Bohlander (2007), p. 415.

114 Gross (2007), esp. p. 4; for a reply see Herring (2007).

a genuine aversion to engaging in sexual activity with brunettes yet does not say anything, Person B is very unlikely to know that this would be a dealbreaker. Identification and communication of these dealbreakers may even be easier in the metaverse and online spaces more generally. For example, the popular dating app Hinge allows users to display a wide variety of information about themselves, from their gender identity to whether they drink, how often they work out, their political leanings and education level. There would have to be a method of discerning mere preferences from absolute dealbreakers, but there would certainly be a way to communicate this through the digital medium that may be far more intuitive to users of these services than it would in an offline conversation.[115] Equally, an assessment of the reasonableness of D's belief is preferable to an assessment of the validity of V's reasons for not engaging in sexual activity as it better reflects V's engagement of their sexual autonomy.

However, this expansive approach is not without issues. If V can place a condition on *any* attribute of their partner, be that race, gender, hair colour, or even ranking in an online game, then would this not require complete disclosure in online spaces to avoid the commission of a sexual offence? Would it necessitate active disclosure of gender identity, location, marital status, political affiliation, or any other aspect of our lives? If we are to treat our responsibility towards partners of a "fiduciary nature",[116] then this may be what is required. However, making such information publicly available is often dangerous—even more so for vulnerable or minority groups.[117] There is equal concern about how much data we wish to put in the hands of private corporations, especially given recent years plagued with scandals concerning the use and sale of data.[118]

5.5.7 Gender and the Nature of the Sexual Act

In *McNally*,[119] D was born female but lived as a male. D used an online profile under the name of Scott, and met V online. Both were teenagers. The relationship developed over 3 years without D disclosing their gender at birth. Following in-person encounters, during which D digitally penetrated V and performed acts of oral sex, V's mother revealed that D had female genitalia. The court held, not based on s.76 but instead relying on s.74, that deception as to gender was sufficient to vitiate the consent: it was an act of a fundamentally different nature to have a sexual interac-

[115] This would not mean that the absence of a 'dealbreaker' in a profile would be evidence that the dealbreaker did not exist but could be instructive in assessing the reasonableness of D's belief if no other representation was made regarding the existence of the dealbreaker.

[116] Herring (2005), p. 6.

[117] See, for example, Human Rights Watch (2023).

[118] For a number of recent examples, including the highest fine ever imposed on a company for data breaches, see Data Protection Commission (2024).

[119] Supra (n91).

tion with a biological woman than a biological man.[120] This decision has been sharply criticised.[121]

As already discussed,[122] the metaverse can provide a safe space for individuals who face discrimination on account of their gender identity to explore and develop connections. Players online are more likely to make avatars that conform to an idealised version of themselves.[123] Additionally, avatars do not have 'genders' in the same way as humans: our perception of gender and attractiveness is based on their appearance and is, therefore rooted in non-virtual norms carried into the virtual space.[124] Other studies have found that avatars can be beneficial for young trans and gender-diverse individuals' well-being due to their ability to experience in-game gender, which aligns with their identity.[125] This is not to say that individuals must always choose avatars which align with their non-virtual gender identity, but that it can be a powerful tool for many marginalised communities.

Against this background, some criticisms of *McNally* require further consideration. Concerns have been raised over the precise *ratio* of the case, which distinguishes sexual interaction as being of a different 'nature' with a cisgender man from a trans-man.[126] However, as D'Souza highlights, on the narrow physical approach taken in *Lawrence*, the object of V's consent ought only to be concerned with whether she consented to the penetration *by D's* fingers and tongue.[127] Is the "nature" alluded to by the courts inherently linked to the fact that it is female or male fingers in the eyes of the court? If so, can such reasoning be extended to the metaverse to mean that a female controller is fundamentally different to a male controller of an avatar, irrespective of the fact that the external physical interaction will be identical and there is never any direct bodily contact between the two?

The same argument could well be made concerning several other characteristics that have come before the courts. Disease transmission and fertility are other interesting examples. After all, the controller's HIV status or infertility has no bearing on a sexual act in the metaverse in the same way as it would in the non-virtual. Had the fact pattern in *Lawrence* occurred in the metaverse, it may well not have received such criticism. That is not to suggest that in *Lawrence,* there was no deception, but that we may have to reframe deceptions as to the 'nature' of the offence in metasexual interactions.[128]

---

[120] *Ibid*, at para [26].

[121] See Sharpe (2014) and see Sharpe (2017) for an example of a rewritten judgement.

[122] Supra (Gladwin 2024).

[123] Thomas and Johansen (2012).

[124] See further on "Netiquette" above.

[125] See, for example, Morgan et al. (2020) and Whitehouse et al. (2023).

[126] [26] does so indirectly, per Sharpe A (n121).

[127] Dsouza (2021), p. 30.

[128] On the expansive reading set out in the previous section, this would not preclude a case whereby V imposes some antiquated or discriminatory condition on their partner (e.g. a refusal to engage in sexual activity with any individual who is HIV positive as a point of principle). If D knew about

Interestingly, the wording of *McNally* frames the issue as one of freedom of choice: V's freedom to choose between sexual activity with a man or a woman has been impeded.[129] A more compelling reading of this judgement focuses on the implications of the deception on V's self-identity: V's perception of their sexuality is an integral part of their identity, and deception having a significant impact on V's identity may preclude the consent given.[130] On this reading, sex-at-birth may remain capable of precluding consent in the metaverse.

The metaverse may also present some reasons to maintain the status of deceptions as to gender and sexuality as capable of precluding consent. Whilst online spaces can be empowering for the LGBTQ+ community, they are also vulnerable to exploitation. In some countries, apps such as Grindr[131] have been monopolised by police forces to entrap individuals and subject them to online extortion, harassment and arrest.[132] Equally, there has been a rise in fetishisation of LGBTQ+ identities, primarily by heterosexual men.[133] For example, say a 40-year-old cisgender man uses a female avatar and targets people who identify as lesbian in a metaverse specifically designed for LGBTQ+ sexual interaction and romantic connections purporting to be a 24-year-old woman. Considering the current case law relating to impersonation and causing unwanted sexual activity online, this is unlikely to fall into this section as D is likely to have gained some form of sexual gratification alongside the intended humiliation or objectification. However, V has evidently been deceived into a sexual encounter contrary to their clearly stated preferences. D knows or reasonably should have known that a lesbian woman would likely not have consented to sexual activity with a cisgender man.

There is an urgent need for further research and understanding of the way that the criminal justice system interacts with the LGBTQ+ community.[134] This is only amplified by both the opportunities and dangers presented for minority and vulnerable communities online.

The following section is a short overview of how the law may deal with the issues highlighted in the preceding discussion. It firstly addresses a form of reintroduction of s.3 of the 1956 procurement offence. The second turns to a potential sustained deception offence.

---

this condition or reasonably ought to have known about it, consent is still likely to have been vitiated.

[129] Supra (Palmer 2021), p. 77.

[130] Kennedy (2021b), p. 101.

[131] Dating app designed for LGBTQ+ sexual encounters and relationships.

[132] Supra (n117).

[133] Anzani et al. (2021) and Rogerson (2022).

[134] It may be that some concerns can be mitigated by procedural changes, such as the treatment of the cases by the CPS. For an overview of current measures taken, see Sharpe (2024).

5.6 Moving Forwards

5.6.1 A Procurement of Deception Offence

As mentioned in Chapter Four, the SOA 2003 notably omitted an equivalent for the 1956 provision concerning the procurement of a woman by false pretences.[135] It has been suggested by others that reintroducing such a provision may be beneficial.[136] The Criminal Law Reform Network has proposed changes to the wording to make the provision gender-neutral, and it ought to be reformulated in line with the proposals in Chap. 4 as regards the type of principal sexual offences it may cover. Whether it is introduced as its own provision or as a series of provisions is still contested.[137] Overall, the law may benefit from some form of separate deception-based offence, even if its primary purpose is to clarify or make coherent existing law.

5.6.2 Sustained Identity Deception Offence

One of the primary issues that may be faced in virtual reality is the possibility of long-term deception through "catfishing". One concern about criminalising long-term deceptive relationships under the principal sexual offences is that, if perpetrated over years, an individual may find themselves faced with innumerable charges. However, the victim has still suffered a serious wrong and undergone a prolonged erosion of her sexual autonomy.[138] Cases such as *Monica* and stories such as Renae Marsden's are unfortunately not one-offs.[139]

The introduction of a sustained deception offence is not a novel proposal. Derry and Palmer, for example, separately argue in favour of a similar offence.[140] The primary arguments in favour consider the consent given in the context of a wider relationship and the potential difference in expectations of candour between a single, casual encounter and other relationships, irrespective of their length.[141] Whilst fact patterns such as *Monica* are not exclusively focused on the sexual act, they are part of the wider narrative in the relationship. Sexual autonomy ought to be considered beyond the physical act in this context. Indeed, continuing and cumulative

[135] The 1956 provision read: 'It is an offence for a person to procure a woman, by false pretences or false representations, to have unlawful sexual intercourse in any part of the world.'

[136] Supra (Child et al. 2022), pp. 493–494.

[137] Gibson (2020), esp. at pp. 99–104.

[138] *Ibid.*

[139] Evans (2024).

[140] Derry (2021), pp. 21–22; supra (Palmer 2021), pp. 78–79 referring to 'Chronic Sexual Violation'.

[141] *Ibid.*

conduct is viewed that way in the context of controlling and coercive behaviour, contrary to s.76 of the Serious Crime Act 2015.[142]

The law ought to be responsive to types of deception and disregard for sexual autonomy that can arise in new contexts, particularly how they can be facilitated by new and developing technologies. A sustained deception offence, applied to repeated violations of sexual autonomy in the context of false offline and online relationships, ought to be considered.

5.7 Conclusion

Overall, it is interesting how many of the core cases found in textbooks already involve offences associated with technology: in *Devonald* and *Bingham,* the offence is facilitated through the medium of technology, in *Jheeta, McNally* and *Lawrence,* the deception, at least in part, arises during online interaction between V and D. Parallels can equally be drawn between *Monica*, and long term catfishing in cases similar to Renae Marsdon's.

This chapter has explored some of the issues which may arise regarding consent to sexual relations in the metaverse. It is by no means an exhaustive analysis. The current issues will likely transpose themselves and, in some cases, be exacerbated by sexual interaction in the metaverse. There is an urgent need for clarity in this area of the law.

References

Aguerri JC et al (2023) Consensus on community guidelines: an experimental study on the legitimacy of content removal in social media. Palgrave Communications, Palgrave Macmillan 10(1):1–11. https://doi.org/10.1057/s41599-023-01917-2

Alencar T (2021) Conditional consent and sexual crime: time for reform? J Criminal Law 85(6):455–465

Anzani A et al (2021) "Being talked to like I was a sex toy, like being transgender was simply for the enjoyment of someone Else": Fetishisation and Sexualisation of transgender and non-binary individuals. Archiv Sex Behav 50(3):897–911. https://doi.org/10.1007/s10508-021-01935-8

Boellstorff T (2020) The ability of place. Curr Anthropol 61:S109–S122. https://doi.org/10.1086/704924

Bohlander M (2007) Mistaken consent to sex, political correctness and correct policy. J Criminal Law 71(5):412–426

Chiesa L (2017) Solving the riddle of rape-by-deception. Yale Law Policy Rev 35(2):407–460

Child JJ et al (2022) Simester and Sullivan's criminal law: theory and doctrine. Hart, Oxford

Conversations on Consent (2022). https://conversationsonconsent.com/wp-content/uploads/2022/09/Legal-Council-v9_03.08.2022.pdf

[142] *Ibid.*

Coroners Court of New South Wales (2020) Findings of inquest into the death of Renae Marsdon. https://coroners.nsw.gov.au/coroners-court/download.html/documents/findings/2020/MARSDEN_Renae_2013-333799_Findings_given_By_Mag_Truscott_DSC_on_20_May_20.pdf
Criminal Law Reform Now Network (2021) Reforming the Relationship between Sexual Consent, Deception and Mistake
Crown Prosecution Service (2021) Rape and Sexual Offences—Chapter 6: Consent. https://www.cps.gov.uk/legal-guidance/rape-and-sexual-offences-chapter-6-consent
Data Protection Commission (2024) Annual Report 2023. https://www.dataprotection.ie/sites/default/files/uploads/2024-08/DPC-EN-AR-2023-Final-AC.pdf
Dawson J (2018) Who is That? The Study of Anonymity and Behavior. https://www.psychologicalscience.org/observer/who-is-that-the-study-of-anonymity-and-behavior#:~:text=The%20hooded%20participants%20were%20twice,faces%20and%20names%20are%20hidden
Derry C (2021) Sustained identity deceptions. In: Criminal law reform now report. Reforming the relationship between sexual consent, deception and mistake, pp 15–23
Dougherty T (2013a) No way around consent: a reply to Rubenfeld on rape-by-deception. Yale Law J Online 123:321. www.yalelawjournal.org/forum/no-way-around-consent-a-reply-to-rubenfeld-on-rape-by-deception
Dougherty T (2013b) Sex lies and consent. Ethics 123(4):717–744
Dreger A (2010) Of Kinks, Crimes and Kinds: The Paraphilias Proposal for the DSM-5. https://www.thehastingscenter.org/of-kinks-crimes-and-kinds-the-paraphilias-proposal-for-the-dsm-5/
Dsouza M (2021) False beliefs and consent to sex. In: Criminal law reform now report (2021) reforming the relationship between sexual consent, deception and mistake, pp 40–47
Dwivedi YK et al (2023) Exploring the Darkverse: a multi-perspective analysis of the negative societal impacts of the Metaverse. Information Sys Front 25:2071–2114. https://doi.org/10.1007/s10796-023-10400-x
Dyson M (2021) Redefining sexual conditions. In: Criminal law reform now report (2021) reforming the relationship between sexual consent, deception and mistake, pp 40–47
Eurostat (2024) Digital Skills in 2023: Impact of Education and Age. https://ec.europa.eu/eurostat/web/products-eurostat-news/w/ddn-20240222-1#:~:text=Lower%20digital%20skills%20were%20recorded,69%25%20compared%20with%2034%25)
Evans R (2024) Police spy 'bragged' about fathering a child with activist, inquiry hears. https://www.theguardian.com/uk-news/2024/oct/14/police-spy-bragged-about-fathering-a-child-with-activist-inquiry-hears
Farah R (2023) Rereading identity deception in the UK sexual offences act 2003. Springer, Cham
Fauchoux V, Bruguière J (2024) Are you ready to protect your digital avatar? https://www.ddg.fr/actualite/are-you-ready-to-protect-your-digital-avatar
Gibson M (2020) Deceptive sexual relations: a theory of criminal liability. Oxf J Leg Stud 40(1):82–109. https://doi.org/10.1093/ojls/gqz031
Gladwin R (2024) Trans people are turning to VR as society fails them. https://mashable.com/article/trans-people-are-turning-to-virtual-reality-as-society-fails-them?test_uuid=01iI2GpryXngy77uIpA3Y4B&test_variant=a
Golovina A (2017) Everybody Lies: What people are lying about on dating sites. https://www.kaspersky.co.uk/blog/online-dating-lies/11880/
Gross H (2007) Rape, moralism and human rights. Criminal Law Rev 3:220–227
Heitmayer M (2023) Netiquette as Digital Social Norms. Int J Human-Comp Interaction 40(13):3334–3354. https://doi.org/10.1080/10447318.2023.2188534
Herring J (2005) Mistaken Consent. Criminal Law Rev, pp 511–524
Herring J (2007) Human rights and rape: a reply to Hyman Gross. Criminal Law Rev March:228–231
Herring J (2009) Relational autonomy and rape. In: Day Sclater S et al (eds) Regulating autonomy: sex, reproduction and family. Bloomsbury Publishing, London. Ch.4

Herring J (2021) Consent Mistaken. In: Criminal law reform now report (2021) reforming the relationship between sexual consent, deception and mistake, pp 56–62
Human Rights Watch (2023) "All This Terror Because of a Photo" Digital Targeting and Its Offline Consequences for LGBT People in the Middle East and North Africa. https://www.hrw.org/report/2023/02/21/all-terror-because-photo/digital-targeting-and-its-offline-consequences-lgbt
Hurd H (1996) The moral magic of consent. Legal Theory 2(2):121–146
Information Commissioners Office (n.d.) Age-appropriate design: A code of practice for online services. Policies and Community standards. https://ico.org.uk/for-organisations/uk-gdpr-guidance-and-resources/childrens-information/childrens-code-guidance-and-resources/age-appropriate-design-a-code-of-practice-for-online-services/6-policies-and-community-standards/
Internet Matters (2018) New survey shows 1 in 5 children are happy to have an "online only" romance. https://www.internetmatters.org/hub/news-blogs/new-survey-shows-1-in-5-children-are-happy-to-have-an-online-only-romance/
Kennedy C (2021a) Sex, selfhood and deception. In: Criminal law reform now report (2021) reforming the relationship between sexual consent, deception and mistake, pp 59–69
Kennedy C (2021b) Criminalising deceptive sex: sex identity and recognition. Leg Stud 41(1):91–110
Kennedy C (2024) Inducing intimacy: deception, consent and the law. Cambridge University Press
Kim M et al (2023) Anonymity and its role in digital aggression: a systematic review. Aggress Violent Behav 72. https://doi.org/10.1016/j.avb.2023.101856
Le Forestier J, Lewis N (2024) When and why people conceal their identities. Nat Rev Psychol 3:489–498. https://doi.org/10.1038/s44159-024-00324-x
Mackinnon C (2016) Rape redefined. Harv Law Policy Rev 10(2):431–477
Mamak K (2023) Cyber banishment: an old sanction for virtual spaces. Crim Justice Stud 36(2):133–145. https://doi.org/10.1080/1478601X.2023.2188449
McQue K (2024) Meta revokes job offer to sextortion expert after he publicly criticises Instagram. https://www.theguardian.com/technology/2024/nov/22/meta-revokes-job-offer-to-sextortion-expert-after-he-publicly-criticises-instagram
Ministry of Justice (2024) Implement affirmative consent for sexual activity response. https://petition.parliament.uk/petitions/657094?reveal_response=yes
Morgan H et al (2020) The role of the avatar in gaming fro trans and gender diverse young people. Int J Environ Res Public Health 17(22). https://doi.org/10.3390/ijerph17228617
National Crime Agency (2024) NCA issues urgent warning about 'sextortion' https://www.nationalcrimeagency.gov.uk/news/nca-issues-urgent-warning-about-sextortion
New York State Senate (2023) Senate Bill S7694A.
North London Coroner's Service (2022) Molly Russell—Prevention of Future Deaths Report. https://www.judiciary.uk/wp-content/uploads/2022/10/Molly-Russell-Prevention-of-future-deaths-report-2022-0315_Published.pdf
Palmer T (2021) Freedom to negotiate. In: Criminal law reform now report (2023) reforming the relationship between sexual consent, deception and mistake, pp 74–83
Raiken A (2024) Nearly half of Gen Z lives a 'double life' online, report finds. https://www.independent.co.uk/life-style/gen-z-online-double-life-b2553975.html
Rogerson R (2022) The Fetishisation or Hyper-Sexualisation of Lesbians and Queer Women. https://the-fword.org.uk/2022/03/the-fetishisation-or-hyper-sexualisation-of-lesbians-and-queer-women/
Rubenfeld J (2013) The riddle of rape-by-deception and the myth of sexual autonomy. Yale Law J 122(6):1372–1443
Sharpe A (2014) Criminalising sexual intimacy: transgender defendants and the legal construction of non-consent. Criminal Law Rev 3:207–223
Sharpe A (2017) Queering judgment: the case of gender identity fraud. J Criminal Law 81(5):417–435. https://doi.org/10.1177/0022018317728828

Sharpe A (2024) 'Deception as to gender': a review of proposed revisions to CPS legal guidance on rape and serious sexual offences. *The*. J Criminal Law. https://doi.org/10.1177/00220183241283223
Thomas AG, Johansen MK (2012) Inside out: avatars as an indirect measure of ideal body self preservation in females. Cyberpyschol J Psychosoc Res Cyberspace 6(3):Article 3
Whitehouse K et al (2023) Trans* and gender diverse players: Avatars and gender-alignment. Entertain Computing 47. https://doi.org/10.1016/j.entcom.2023.100584
Yee N, Bailenson J (2007) The Proteus effect: the effect of transformed self-representation on behaviour. Hum Commun Res 33(3):271–290. https://doi.org/10.1111/j.1468-2958.2007.00299.x
YouGov (2018) Public's Attitudes to Sexual Consent. https://yougov.co.uk/society/articles/22262-publics-attitudes-sexual-consent
YouGov (2022) Unlocking the Metaverse. https://www.iab.com/wp-content/uploads/2022/10/Metaverse-8.22.pdf
Zimbardo P (1969) The human choice: individuation, reason, and order verses deindividuation, impulse and chaos. Neb Symp Motiv 17:237–307

Chapter 6
Contextualising the Argument

6.1 Introduction

Having outlined the legal arguments in favour of the criminalisation of sexual offences in the metaverse in the previous chapters, this chapter now turns to situate those arguments within criminal law and society more broadly. It will begin with a discussion on the wider impacts of this argument for domestic law, with a particular focus on the Offences Against the Person Act 1861 and the Theft Act 1968. It will follow by briefly considering what impact this argument may have on the legal status of private entities which own and maintain metaverses. Finally, it will seek to place these arguments within the wider context of technological innovation and argue that we must reject the view that technology is inherently 'neutral'.

6.2 Wider Impacts on Domestic Law

The analysis presented in the preceding chapters cannot exist in a vacuum. An expansion of the law on sexual offences to virtual reality would require a similar approach in other areas of the law. This section will focus on two in particular: the Offences Against the Person Act 1861 and the Theft Act 1968.

R. Procktor, *The Sexual Offences Act 2003 and Virtual Reality*, SpringerBriefs in Law, https://doi.org/10.1007/978-3-032-10397-0_6

6.2.1 *The Offences Against the Person Act 1861 and Common Law Offences Against the Person*

It is unsurprising, given the parallels drawn in previous chapters, that I advocate for the application of the OAPA 1861 in the metaverse. An almost identical analysis of common law assault and battery can be made in a non-sexual context. There should be little issue with identifying bodily harm both in the external, narrow sense and in the expansive sense, as recognised in *Chan-Fook* and confirmed in *Ireland*.[1] As a result, assault causing actual and grievous bodily harm will also be possible. Whether such an analysis could be extended to form the basis of a manslaughter or murder charge is not as clear. Certainly, were Person A to punch in the virtual world Person B, the perception of it causing them to lose their balance, fall and succumb to fatal injuries, then a charge of constructive manslaughter may be plausible. I would not go as far as to say that this is evident: further research and consideration of these issues in greater depth is necessary.

Equally, this argument does not advocate a wholesale adoption of the OAPA in the metaverse—there are many areas where current sections could never apply.[2] Further, there must be consideration over the types of behaviour that will be excluded from criminal liability. It has long been recognised that sportspeople, for example, may consent to a higher level of bodily contact than others.[3] Whilst it has both clearly and consistently been held that it is not in the public interest for individuals to try and cause each other bodily harm for no good reason, the law has carved out certain exceptions in sports and 'rough horseplay'.[4] Returning to the comment made following reports of a police investigation into a rape in the metaverse set out at the beginning of this book, we may be in a good place to start giving reasons as to why a sexual assault in the metaverse is worth criminalisation, whereas being killed in Call of Duty is not.[5] The limits of a "gaming" exception to battery merit consideration, particularly as relates to the potential infliction of actual and grievous bodily harm. However, I imagine that some form of exception would exist, the question is more as to how this is defined and where the boundaries are drawn.

---

[1] [1994] 1 WLR 689, at p.695 per Lord Hobhouse: "T*he body of the victim includes all parts of his body, including his organs, his nervous system and his brain. Bodily injury therefore may include injury to any of those parts of his body responsible for his mental and other faculties.*", confirmed in R v Ireland [1997] UKHL 34.

[2] For example, s.24 Offences Against the Person Act relating to poisoning.

[3] AG Ref. No. 6 of 1980 [1981] QB 715.

[4] *Ibid*; where it was held that games and sports, lawful chastisement or correction, reasonable surgical interference and dangerous exhibitions did not entail criminal liability. This was not an exhaustive list; see further, R v Barnes [2004] EWCA Crim 3246 at [15]; "*The type of the sport, the level at which it is played, the nature of the act, the degree of force used, the extent of the risk of injury, the state of mind of the defendant are all likely to be relevant in determining whether the defendant's actions go beyond the threshold [required to impose criminal liability]*".

[5] "I was killed in Call of Duty, been waiting for my killer to be brought to justice."

6.2.2 The Theft Act 1968

In 2012, the Dutch Supreme Court upheld a conviction for the robbery of an enchanted mask and a magic amulet in the popular game Runescape.[6] The D's went to V's house[7] and quickly became violent. V subsequently logged onto the game and made his avatar drop the items, allowing one of the offender's avatars to pick them up.[8] The Court concluded that the fact that the items were virtual did not preclude them from being able to be stolen.[9] This was held irrespective of the fact that the rules of the game stipulated that individuals cannot 'own' objects themselves: all objects are part of the game's internal economy and, therefore, may belong to the game's owners.[10]

The question of whether purely virtual items can be stolen is growing in importance, especially in the era of cryptocurrency—which is likely to play a large role in commercial enterprises and assets in the metaverse.[11] Such questions are especially salient in a context where non-virtual crimes are committed to obtain possession of digital assets, such as the case described above and in 'rubber hose attacks' on owners of Bitcoin, which have been growing in frequency since 2015.[12]

There may, however, be a greater issue with theft occurring exclusively in the metaverse. Such an analysis may vary in each digital space, depending on the rules of ownership and how assets are traded in a specific virtual context. However, there is no initial reason as to why virtual assets should not be capable of being stolen, especially in the interoperable and proprietary context of the metaverse. However, as has already been noted concerning cryptocurrency, such an analysis raises several questions on the interpretation of the Theft Act which are deserving of greater attention.[13]

6.2.3 Further Impacts

The two potential implications of my argument in relation to sexual offences outlined above are by no means exhaustive. Indeed, international policing bodies have identified an array of crimes that could be perpetrated in the metaverse, including

[6] RuneScape theft, Supreme Court of the Netherlands LJN: BQ9251, Hoge Raad, 10/00101 J.

[7] In the non-virtual world.

[8] Lodder (2013), p. 3.

[9] *Ibid.* p. 4.

[10] *Ibid.*

[11] On the issues surrounding ownership and identification of assets in the metaverse, see Wyczik (2024).

[12] Taylor et al. (2021), p. 2.

[13] *Ibid*, esp. at p. 25.

terrorism offences, fraud, and harassment.[14] Issues surrounding applications of criminal law at these new virtual frontiers merit close attention from the academic and law enforcement communities.

6.3 A Third Party?

Criminal law generally encompasses the punishment of individuals by the state, primarily justified by the need to prevent individual actions from negatively impacting society. However, in the context of the metaverse, we face more complex issues as to jurisdiction and the role of the state in spaces created and largely "governed" by international companies. In recent years, there has been a trend towards viewing social media companies as "digital public squares"[15] or debating their status as publishers with editorial discretion or as mere intermediaries for different forms of speech.[16] These debates often arise concerning freedom of expression and the role played by large social media companies in either promoting or restricting free speech.

However, as noted in this book, there is a clear distinction between communications offences and restriction of free speech with the type of immersed, physical offences possible in the metaverse. A metaverse where a single company or group write and enforces the rules governing interactions between individuals and with the governing entity bears more resemblance to criminal law than it does to contract. Certainly, the powers of large social media companies are beginning to appear closer to the coercive powers usually present in state entities—without most (if not all) of the internal judicial and political scrutiny![17] The virtual world, perhaps even specific virtual worlds created by individual companies, are beginning to align closely with what may at first glance appear to be a jurisdiction in and of itself. Whether or not specific metaverses could become their own jurisdiction, or whether the metaverse itself is a jurisdiction, is a complicated question not readily lending itself to one specific area of law, and I will not attempt to answer it here. However, it is worth noting that there must be greater discussion on the role of private for-profit actors in this space. It is not unreasonable to suggest that they may have some form of "quasi-jurisdiction"; in a space where users are not just communicating but are physically interacting, their role seems to go beyond mere publishers and facilitators of dialogue.

---

[14] Europol (2022) and Interpol (2024).

[15] Packham v. North Carolina 582 U.S. 98 (2017), p. 8.

[16] See, for example, NetChoice, LLC v. Paxton, 600 U.S. ___ 2024.

[17] Kastelein (2021).

6.4 The Wider Context

I mentioned in Chap. 3 the concept of relational concept of autonomy, and implicit in much of my reasoning (and at times rather explicit!) is this belief that our individual capacity to make decisions is embedded within our social relationships.[18] Increasingly frequently, these social relationships are facilitated and sometimes originate through technology, be that through email, social media, or indeed the metaverse.

As has been stressed throughout this book, interactions online do not take place within a vacuum but are heavily reliant on social norms and power structures already in existence. Whilst technology has the potential to radically transform society, it is also prone to confirming existing biases and power structures. There is an underpinning thread as to why most digitised care labour has been programmed to be female,[19] ChatGPT writes more positive letters of recommendation for men than for women,[20] and a recent UN report highlighted the ways that the use of AI is actively contributing to manifestations of racial discrimination.[21] This is not unsurprising from a design standpoint, considering the stereotype of engineering and computer science as quasi-exclusively male domains.[22]

There is a broader push to view emerging technologies as 'neutral', as clay to be moulded and shaped by all communities. This could not be further from the truth. The assumption that new technologies are somehow free from the social values of the rest of society is unrealistic, especially considering they are created by and used as tools of that same society in pursuit of profit for a small and overwhelmingly white, heterosexual male elite.

We ought not to buy into the 'neutral' assumption and recognise the wider social and technological context in which interactions occur, encouraging diversity in the design and implementation of these technologies. There are ways of developing inclusive technologies which can create online spaces where social power structures from the non-virtual can be diminished. However, these practices are not yet widespread.

I mention the above as it is important to contextualise sexual interactions in the metaverse and online more generally. Technology is not neutral, and many of the biases that exist in the non-virtual remain and are at times amplified, perhaps in part due to the perception of anonymity and lack of repercussions.[23]

---

[18] This phrasing is borrowed from Delgado (2019).

[19] Rhee (2023).

[20] Kaplan et al. (2024).

[21] Ashwini (2024).

[22] Wajcman and Young (2023), p. 48.

[23] See the discussions on the Proteus Effect in Ch2 and comments on the prevalence of deception in Chap. 4.

Increased legal and interdisciplinary discussion of the issues arising from new technologies will be vital in helping to forge the path ahead inclusively and collaboratively. It is hoped that this book will in some way contribute to that.

References

Ashwini KP (2024) Report of the Special Rapporteur on contemporary forms of racism, racial discrimination, xenophobia and related intolerance. A/HRC/56/68. https://documents.un.org/doc/undoc/gen/g24/084/20/pdf/g2408420.pdf

Delgado (2019) Re-thinking relational autonomy: challenging the triumph of autonomy through vulnerability. Bioethics Update 5(1):50–65

Europol (2022) Policing in the Metaverse: What Law Enforcement Needs to Know. https://www.europol.europa.eu/cms/sites/default/files/documents/Policing%20in%20the%20metaverse%20-%20what%20law%20enforcement%20needs%20to%20know.pdf

Interpol (2024) Metaverse: A Law Enforcement Perspective. https://www.interpol.int/en/News-and-Events/News/2024/Grooming-radicalization-and-cyber-attacks-INTERPOL-warns-of-Metacrime

Kaplan D et al (2024) What's in a name? Experimental evidence of gender bias in recommendation letters generated by ChatGPT. J Med Internet Res 26:e51837

Kastelein N (2021) Big Tech: private companies now wielding the coercive power of government like a one-party state. https://www.spectator.com.au/2021/01/big-tech-private-companies-now-wielding-the-coercive-power-of-government-like-a-one-party-state/

Lodder A (2013) Dutch supreme court 2012 : virtual theft ruling a one-off or first in a series? J Virtual Worlds Res 6(3):1–12

Rhee J (2023) From ELIZA to Alexa : automated care labour and the otherwise of radical care. In: Browne J et al (eds) Feminist AI: critical perspectives on algorithms, data, and intelligent machines, pp 155–173

Taylor A, Floinn Ó, M. (2021) Bitcoin burglaries and the theft act 1968. Criminal Law Rev 2021(3):163–190

Wajcman J, Young E (2023) Feminism confronts AI : the gender relations of digitalisation. In: Browne J et al (eds) Feminist AI: critical perspectives on algorithms, data, and intelligent machines, pp 47–64

Wyczik J (2024) The rise of the Metaverse: tethering effect and intellectual property of crypto tokens. J Intellect Property Law Practice 19(4):358–370

Chapter 7
Conclusion

This book has considered some of the potential implications of metaverse technology for the English and Welsh law on sexual offences. It is clear that there is much work to be done, both in relation to the material discussed here and the law more broadly.

It has sought to provide an overview of the technology as it stands and—as far as possible—where it is going. On this basis, this book has argued that the current provisions of the Sexual Offences Act 2003 are broadly underdeveloped and ill-equipped to address the specific types of acts that can be facilitated by metaverse technology. It has explored some offences that could be enacted to promote safe and equitable experiences in immersive virtual reality, including most notably, sexual assault (including sexual assault and sexual battery), rape by penetration and constructive rape. I am aware that the provisions suggested are broad and expand the current scope of criminalisation. However, I do not believe that this is unmerited. If we are serious about protecting individuals and their autonomy, then reform is necessary, and it will likely have to expand the scope of criminalisation to encompass new forms of criminal behaviour which can be facilitated by technology.

Another area desperately requiring more attention is the state of the law on consent. The fine lines drawn by the common law are not only difficult to apply in the

R. Procktor, *The Sexual Offences Act 2003 and Virtual Reality*, SpringerBriefs in Law, https://doi.org/10.1007/978-3-032-10397-0_7

non-virtual but nearly impossible in the online space where deception is not only tolerated but at times expected. Equally, the law must grapple with a difficult balancing act between ensuring the validity of consent and the privacy of each of the parties. Even questions surrounding relatively non-controversial aspects of the law are already being raised, and we should expect such tensions to continue.[1] This book has further argued in favour of the reintroduction of a deception offence and the potential inclusion of a further sustained deception offence.

Finally, this book has argued that, although taking this position in respect of the Sexual Offences Act 2003 does necessitate changes in other areas of the criminal law, such changes are not implausible. They do, however, merit much deeper consideration and analysis. Equally, this book has left open the questions of jurisdiction and the role of large multinational corporations: the analysis in this book is limited to the extent that it could only be applied in the courts of England and Wales.

There are three final overarching points I wish to make. Firstly, that it is important to look backwards to look forward. Many of the complexities and unresolved issues present in the current law are exacerbated in the metaverse, and in order not to entrench them further, we must recognise these issues and address them. The law must take stock of the reality of modern society: social, professional and romantic relationships are increasingly facilitated by technology, and children and young people are often far more technologically minded and literate than other generations. They are exposed to a widely different array of harms than their predecessors, which the law ought to be equipped to deal with.

Secondly, this is not a change that can be realised only by the law and legal academics. Interdisciplinary collaboration and research are more important now than ever, and it will take a convergence of lawyers, philosophers, scientists, and policymakers to start to forge different ways of addressing the issues we are, and indeed will, face.

Finally, although it is important to recognise the dangers presented by new technologies such as the metaverse, we ought also to be optimistic about them. The metaverse shows great promise, and there are ways that it can be used to improve the lives of users and society more generally.

This book will end with a call to recognise these positive benefits and to develop regulatory and other legal mechanisms to ensure that such benefits are realised in a safe, equitable and sustainable way.

[1] See for example the discussion on impersonation and what it means to know someone 'personally' for the purposes of s.76 Sexual Offences Act 2003, or the same question as assessed under s.74.

MIX
Papier aus verantwortungsvollen Quellen
Paper from responsible sources
FSC® C105338

If you have any concerns about our products,
you can contact us on
ProductSafety@springernature.com

In case Publisher is established outside the EU,
the EU authorized representative is:
Springer Nature Customer Service Center GmbH
Europaplatz 3, 69115 Heidelberg, Germany

Printed by Libri Plureos GmbH
in Hamburg, Germany